A CANOEING AND KAYAKING GUIDE TO KENTUCKY

OTHER CANOEING AND KAYAKING GUIDES

BY MENASHA RIDGE PRESS

A Canoeing and Kayaking Guide to the Carolinas

A Canoeing and Kayaking Guide to Florida

A Canoeing and Kayaking Guide to Georgia

A Canoeing and Kayaking Guide to the Ozarks

A Canoeing and Kayaking Guide to West Virginia

A CANOEING AND KAYAKING GUIDE TO KENTUCKY

Bob Sehlinger *and* Johnny Molloy

Fifth Edition

MENASHA RIDGE PRESS
Birmingham, Alabama

DEDICATION

This book is for all the paddlers of Kentucky—from those on the waters of Land Between the Lakes, to the steep creeks of central Kentucky, to the casual floaters on the Licking, to the float fishermen on the Green, to the canoe campers on the Big South Fork, to those floating the entire length of the Kentucky River, to the those on the Elkhorn on a Sunday afternoon— may you keep on stroking in the Bluegrass.

Copyright © 2004 by Bob Sehlinger and Johnny Molloy
All rights reserved
Published by Menasha Ridge Press
Printed in the United States of America
Distributed by The Globe Pequot Press
Fifth edition, first printing

Library of Congress Cataloging-in-Publication Data:

Sehlinger, Bob, 1945–
A canoeing & kayaking guide to the streams of Kentucky/ by Bob Sehlinger and Johnny Molloy.
p. cm.
Rev. ed. of: A canoeing and kayaking guide to the streams of Kentucky. c1994.

ISBN 0-89732-565-6

1. Canoes and canoeing—Kentucky—Guidebooks. 2. Kayaking—Kentucky—Guidebooks. 3. White-water canoeing—Kentucky—Guidebooks. 4. Kentucky—Tours. I. Title: Canoeing and kayaking guide to the streams of Kentucky. II. Molloy, Johnny, 1961— III. Sehlinger, Bob, 1945— Canoeing and kayaking guide to the streams of Kentucky. IV. Title.

[GV776.K4S43 2004]
797.7'22'09769--dc22

2003071063

Cover photo by Alan Baldwin
Cover design by Bud Zehmer
Text design by Ann Marie Healy
Cartography by Peggy Gordon

Table *of* Contents

part**One**

STREAMS OF THE EASTERN COAL FIELDS

part**Two**

THE LICKING RIVER AND ITS TRIBUTARIES

part**Three**

THE KENTUCKY RIVER AND ITS TRIBUTARIES

part**Four**

CREEK DRAINAGES OF MADISON COUNTY

part**Five**

THE CUMBERLAND RIVER AND ITS TRIBUTARIES

part**Six**

THE SALT RIVER SYSTEM OF THE WESTERN BLUEGRASS

part**Seven**

HEADWATERS OF THE GREEN RIVER

part**Eight**

STREAMS OF THE WESTERN COAL FIELDS

part**Nine**

STREAMS OF LAND BETWEEN THE LAKES

part**Ten**

STREAMS OF THE JACKSON PURCHASE

part**Eleven**

WATERS OF SPECIAL MENTION

Appendices

Map List

acknowledgments

Thanks to Greg Woosley for helping with the Jessamine Creek and Hickman Creek write-ups. Dedicated paddlers like him strengthen whitewater boating all around. A special thanks to Barry Grimes and Don Spangler for helping us with much of the Kentucky whitewater from beginning to end and for offering insight into the ever-changing state of paddling. Thanks to American Whitewater and Scott Collins for their help, to Jim Thaxton for showing us around the Licking River watershed, to Ed Council for his help on the Elkhorn, to Alice Rankin for her help on Four Mile Creek, to Bradley Monton for his insight, and to Mark Branch for his paddling expertise. Thanks to Lisa Daniel for going canoeing with us on the Green, to Steve Grayson for paddling the South Fork Licking, and to John Cox for paddling in the Big South Fork. Thanks to Ben Culbertson for guiding us around the Red River Gorge. Also, thanks to all the folks at Menasha Ridge Press for making this book happen.

A CANOEING AND KAYAKING GUIDE TO KENTUCKY

introduction

Canoeing and kayaking rivals horses and basketball as a way of life for Kentuckians. Okay, that may be an exaggeration. Nevertheless, paddling the Bluegrass has a rabid following that increases on a yearly basis. The first edition of this book, written by Kentucky native Bob Sehlinger, has become a classic and helped propel paddling to the forefront among outdoor enthusiasts throughout the Commonwealth. Since 1978, untold Kentuckians have used this various editions o this book as a river resource. And as one paddler brought another one into the fold—passing down the paddle if you will—this book has been the standard, opening new rivers and streams to those who ventured forth with excitement that is only found when your boat curves around a new bend of a new stream offering new scenery and new opportunities. As Kentucky outdoor legend Arthur B. Lander, Jr. wrote in the original introduction to this book, whether you are "drifting down a lazy, meandering river, or maneuvering a canoe or kayak through a jumble of boulders on a roller coaster of whitewater, is not only great fun, but a genuine mental and physical challenge. Americans are adventuresome by character, and are quick to seek the exhilaration that only life in the outdoors can bring."

That statement is no less true today than it was back then. Since this book was first printed, a whole new class of paddlers has emerged, the "steep creekers." These people paddle small creeks with limited drainages that flow perhaps a dozen times per year, taking hair-raising trips and challenging the heretofore limits of the Kentucky whitewater realm. Advances and variations in boat designs have gone far beyond what paddlers of the 1970s could have even imagined. Today we have modern canoes of varied plastic composites that range from heavily rockered whitewater boats to long and deep touring boats designed for extended trips. And kayaks have changed more. Today we have bombproof boats designed for maneuvering heavy whitewater and short, squat "play boats" used by paddlers to "surf" one single rapid for hours.

This book attempts to inform paddlers of paddling opportunities in the Bluegrass State, especially as the sport has advanced and many new streams are being explored. New watercourses have been added to this latest edition. This guidebook is the product of scouting miles of river, and hours of map work and research writing. Along the way, many memories were made. We hope you will make some memories of your own, paddling the streams of Kentucky.

The Drainages of Kentucky

All the major rivers in Kentucky flow in a westerly, or northwesterly, direction. From east to west, the major rivers are the Big Sandy, Licking, Kentucky, Salt, Green, Tradewater, Cumberland, and Tennessee. They all empty into the Ohio River, which forms the northern boundary of Kentucky for 664 miles from Catlettsburg on the east to the Mississippi River on the west. About 97 percent of the total area of the commonwealth drains into the Ohio River.

The claim that Kentucky has more miles of running water than any state except Alaska is not unfounded; there are approximately 54,000 miles of streams and rivers when you add up all the major tributaries to the Ohio River, plus Mayfield Creek, Obion Creek and Bayou Du Chien, which drain into the Mississippi River in the far western Jackson Purchase region. The Tennessee River, which empties into the Ohio River at Paducah, is the fifth-largest river system in the United States, with a basin of more than 40,000 square miles occupying portions of seven states (1,055 square miles are in Kentucky alone). The Ohio River at its mouth is exceeded in volume of flow only by the lower Mississippi River. On the average, the Ohio River discharges three times more water than the upper Mississippi River, and about three and one third times more water than the Missouri River. As a point of comparison, the Ohio's volume is about the same as both the Columbia and St. Lawrence rivers, major rivers of the North American continent.

The Cumberland and Green River basins both have considerably more square miles than any one of Kentucky's other five major basins. The Cumberland River basin drains more than 18,000 square miles in Kentucky and Tennessee. The river's headwaters are in extreme southeastern Kentucky (Poor Fork in Letcher County and Martins Fork in Bell County) and its mouth is at Smithland, in Livingston County of western Kentucky. Between the so-called "upper and lower" Cumberland basins, the river flows through Tennessee, where at least half of its basin lies. The Green River and its many tributaries flow across central Kentucky, encompassing more than 9,000 square miles of basin. In decreasing basin size are: the Kentucky River, roughly 6,940 square miles; the Licking River, 3,670 square miles; the Salt River, 2,890 square miles; and finally the Big Sandy River basin at Kentucky's far eastern boundary with 2,280 square miles in Kentucky alone.

The quality of streams in Kentucky is generally good although portions of several drainages are polluted by acid water and washings from coal mines, brine from oil fields, and sewage and industrial wastes. The Levisa Fork of the Big Sandy River is basically a high-quality mountain stream. However, some mine drainage has made the water hard and high in sulfates. The upper Cumberland River also has high-quality water typical of a mountain stream, but it receives much less mine drainage and so is of better quality than Levisa Fork. The Kentucky River drains a limestone area and is typical of many of Kentucky's streams; its water is hard and of the calcium bicarbonate type. The Tradewater River is an example of a small river that contains much acid from iron, manganese, and aluminum compounds, while Mayfield Creek is an example of the excellent water in the Jackson Purchase region.

In general, the water in small creeks in Kentucky is of the highest quality, especially in the mountains, but it is also the easiest to pollute because of the limited flows. Water in the large rivers, such as the Kentucky, Green, Tennessee, and Ohio, is more or less uniform in quality (or lack thereof) because the flows of these rivers tend to decrease the differences in the quality of the water entering from the tributaries.

Seasonal variations in the flow levels of watercourses are based on fluctuations in rainfall. Kentucky's yearly average of 46 inches of rain is equal to about 32 trillion gallons a year for all of Kentucky. About 37 percent of this, or 12 trillion gallons, runs either directly into the streams or through the ground and eventually into the streams. This much water alone would keep the Ohio River flowing for about 70 days at average flow. March and April are Kentucky's rainiest months. An average of 5.05 inches of precipitation a month falls in March, the rainiest month. October is the driest month, with an average of 2.35 inches of precipitation.

Mayfield Creek is in the Jackson Purchase region, a part of the state underlain with thick soils, sands, and gravels. Water stored in these materials during the winter and spring later seeps out to help maintain flow in hot, dry months. In the far eastern coal field region, land slopes are steep, bedrock appears at the surface, and the soil is relatively thin. There is less opportunity and capacity for water storage in the ground.

Localized soil conditions have a great deal to do with stream flow as do plant life, terrain slope, ground cover, and air temperature. In summer, during the peak growing season, water is used more readily by plants, and higher air temperatures encourage increased evaporation. The fall and winter low water periods are caused by decreased precipitation, although since the ground is frozen and plant use of water is for the most part halted abnormally high amounts of rain, or water from melting snow, can cause flash floods because surface runoff is high—there's no place for the water to go but into creeks and rivers. Though surface runoff is first to reach the river, it is groundwater that keeps many larger streams flowing during rainless periods. Drought can lower the water table drastically. Soil erosion is related to surface runoff—hilly land in intensive agricultural use is a prime target for loss of topsoil and flash flooding. The Salt River basin has severe soil erosion that creates continued and increasing chances of flooding. The Barren River basin, a tributary to the Green River, is intensely farmed, but the chance of flooding is less severe since the soil is absorbent and the terrain is relatively flat.

Kentucky Wild Rivers System

Eight Kentucky rivers of exceptional quality and aesthetic character are protected from development by the Wild Rivers System enacted by the Kentucky Legislature. The rivers' rights-of-way are protected from strip mining, the construction of any impoundments, new roads, and buildings, or timber cutting within 2,000 feet of the middle of the watercourses.

The eight rivers, six of which are classic paddling streams, are remote and as unspoiled as any in Kentucky, and have rocky cliffs, sweeping forests and abundant fish and wildlife resources along their free-flowing paths. They are essentially untouched by the works of man, and are rich in recreational opportunity. Their protection is in the hands of Kentucky's Department for Natural Resources and Environmental Protection.

Six of Kentucky's eight wild rivers are in the upper Cumberland basin, one is in the Kentucky River drainage, and one is in the Green River system. There is one wild river in each of Kentucky's two national parks and six in Daniel Boone National Forest (including one in a national geological area in the forest). The wild rivers and their boundaries are:

Cumberland River   6.1 miles, from Summer Shoals to the backwaters of Lake Cumberland, in McCreary and Whitley counties. (1)

Red River   9.1 miles, from the KY 746 bridge to the mouth of Swift Camp Creek, in the Red River Gorge Geological Area; in Wolfe and Powell counties of the Stanton District of Daniel Boone National Forest. (2)

Ohio

West
Virginia

Virginia

Indiana

Tennessee

Illinois

Missouri

1. Cumberland River
2. Red River
3. Rockcastle River
4. Green River
5. Big South Fork of the
   Cumberland River
6. Rock Creek
7. Martins Fork of the
   Cumberland River
8. Little South Fork of the
   Cumberland River

Rockcastle River   15.9 miles of whitewater, from the KY 1956 bridge to the backwaters of Lake Cumberland, in Pulaski and Laurel counties. (3)

Green River   26 miles in the confines of Mammoth Cave National Park; a classic flatwater run with camping allowed on islands or riverside sites, abundant wildlife, and rivers bubbling up from underground caverns. (4)

Big South Fork of the Cumberland River   10.2 miles of one of the most celebrated whitewater runs in the eastern United States, from the Tennessee border to Blue Heron, in Whitley County. (5)

Rock Creek   18 miles of good rainbow trout stream, from the Tennessee border to the White Oak Junction bridge. (6)

Martins Fork of the Cumberland River   3.9 miles of shallow, nonnavigable water extending from the eastern boundary of Cumberland Gap National Historical Park to KY 987. The headwaters of this crystal clear, brook trout–stocked stream are in a grove of virgin hemlock trees. (7)

Little South Fork of the Cumberland River   10.4 miles, from the KY 92 bridge in the backwaters of Lake Cumberland, in Wayne and McCreary counties. (8)

Rating River Difficulty

American Whitewater's River Classification System provides a good framework for discussing river difficulty. However, there are considerable variations in how this system is interpreted nationwide. Some expert paddlers tend to underrate everything, and an inexperienced paddler may go the other way and overestimate the difficulty. What seems horrendous to one person may be quite manageable to a more skilled paddler. If you have any doubts about your ability to handle a run, talk to paddlers who have done it before or allow some extra time to scout.

For years there's been pressure to downgrade rivers in response to innovations in boat design and technique. We have chosen not to do this, thus some rivers and creeks in this guide may seem overrated to expert paddlers. However, do not expect to finesse a "steep creek" like Lower Howard's Creek because you have run Russell Fork a few times! Every year, a number of steeper, more demanding runs are being run and redefine the limits of whitewater sport.

American Whitewater River Classification System

CLASS I—EASY. Occasional small riffles consisting of low, regular wave patterns. About what you might encounter on a lake on a mildly windy day.

CLASS II—MEDIUM DIFFICULTY. Rapids occur more frequently, usually retaining a regular wave pattern as on a lake with a fairly vigorous wind (enough to cause whitecaps). Although there may be more than one route, the most practical one is easily determined. There may be simple, uncomplicated chutes over ledge up to 3 feet high.

CLASS III—DIFFICULT. Numerous rapids, with higher, irregular standing waves, hydraulics, and eddies. In Class III rapids you must maneuver. The most practical route may not be obvious, and you'll find that you have to work a little. Expect ledges up to 4 feet, waves up to 3 feet, overhanging branches, and deeper water.

CLASS IV—MORE DIFFICULT. Long, extensive stretches of rapids with high, irregular standing waves and difficult hydraulics, holes, eddies, and crosscurrents. Good boat control is essential, and you are working very hard. Class IV requires plenty of fast decision making because the most practical route may not be obvious. Difficult ledges with irregular passages, "stopper" waves, or souse holes may block the way.

CLASS V—EXTREMELY DIFFICULT. It's not always easy to tell where Class IV ends and Class V begins. These rapids are not only quite difficult but they are long and continuous. Irregular stoppers and souse holes are unavoidable; partially submerged boulders and ledges are everywhere; very complex eddies and crosscurrents are not only present but occur in long, dazzling combinations. Common usage also refers to short, very intense rapids as Class V if they require a lot of skill and courage to run.

CLASS VI—UTMOST DIFFICULTY. This isn't a hard class to define, but in recent years there's been a tendency to ignore the definition. It's supposed to mean the utmost limit of navigability, with its chief distinguishing characteristic being unusual risk of life. Mistakes made here can be fatal. No one should ever be urged or taunted into running a Class VI rapid.

When the difficulty of a river falls between two grades, two numbers will be used, i.e., Class II–III. If most of the river is of one classification except for one or two spots, it is referred to as, say, Class III(IV). These ratings are for normal water levels, and classifications may change drastically in high water. Similarly, river ratings usually drop about a class in low water. If you run a few Class IVs in low-water conditions, don't assume you are a Class IV paddler.

Using River Gauges

The Water Resources Division of the United States Geological Survey measures water flows on most rivers in the United States at frequent intervals. The United States Army Corps of Engineers and various power companies collect similar information. These flows are recorded in cubic feet per second (cfs) and are available to everyone.

The key variable is the height of the river at a fixed point. Gauge houses, situated on most rivers, consist of a well at the river's edge with a float attached to a recording clock. The gauge reads in hundredths of feet. Rating tables are constructed for each gauge to get a cfs reading for each level.

This information is very useful for paddlers who are planning a trip. In the "old days," paddlers had to phone various government offices and listen to recorded messages. They also contacted outfitters and private individuals who kept track of nearby paddler gauges. Nowadays we can get this information quickly at various Web sites, along with the weather! A few clicks gather information that would have taken us dozens of phone calls to obtain. Multiple Web sites provide backup when a single site goes down.

Water Level Sites

USGS—Real-time Water Levels for Kentucky; http://waterdata.usgs.gov/ky/nwis/rt

The United States Geologic Survey has compiled an in depth Web site. Hundreds of gauges for the entire country are updated continually, and graphs showing recent flow trends are now available at the touch of a mouse. This is the greatest thing for paddlers since spray skirts were invented.

American Whitewater; www.americanwhitewater.org

This site collects USGS gauge readings for whitewater rivers throughout the country and automatically extrapolates water levels on rivers not covered by these gauges. They have an individual section for Kentucky's streams, www.americanwhitewater.org/rivers/state/KY/, that will prove very valuable to paddlers in the Bluegrass State.

WATERLINE SERVICE

Waterline is a free, 24-hour phone service covering most of the USGS gauges mentioned in this book. Their figures are continuously updated every few hours, 24 hours a day, 7 days a week. They can be accessed by phone, without a computer. This is very useful when you are on the road and can't access the Web through your cell phone.

To get a reading, call (800) 452-1737. This gets you into an automated menu; you then dial the code number of the river gauge you want. You will get the current reading and a number of prior readings. For more information, call Waterline at (800) 945-3376 or check their Web site at www.h2oline.com for the site codes of the river and streams about which you are interested.

Hazards and Safety

Hazardous situations likely to be encountered on rivers and creeks must be identified and understood for safe paddling. The lure of high adventure, especially on little-run streams, has in part explained why there are so many more paddlers these days. Unfortunately, an alarming number were not prepared for what they encountered and lost their lives. They didn't use good judgment or just didn't understand the potential dangers. Below are some safety guidelines.

Winter Paddling

Winter paddling can be beautiful. It can also be when the steep creeks are running high. However, winter paddling can also be quite dangerous unless certain precautions are taken. Some rules that should be followed by boaters are:

1. Paddle those streams on which you can walk to shore at any point. It is best to stay off the larger rivers and those nearing flood stage.

2. Always have at least three boats in the party.

3. Everyone should have a complete change of clothing in a waterproof container that will withstand pressures of immersion.

4. Each paddler should carry on his person a supply of matches in a waterproof containter.

5. Remember that the classification of any particular river is automatically upgraded when canoeing in cold weather. This is due to the extreme effects on the body upon immersion in cold water.

Cold-Weather Survival

With more and more paddlers going out in the cold weather to engage in their sport, a basic knowledge of cold water and cold weather survival is necessary. When immersed in water, the loss of heat from the body becomes much more rapid and survival times without suitable clothing in cold water become very short. For instance, wet clothes lose about 90 percent of their insulating value and lose heat 240 times faster than dry clothing.

The following table gives the approximate survival times of humans immersed in water at various temperatures.

Water Temp (°F)	Exhaustion or Unconsciousness	Survival Time
32.5	0–15 min.	0–45 min.
32.5–40	15–30 min.	30–60 min.
40–50	30–60 min.	1–3 hrs.
50–60	1–2 hrs.	1–6 hrs.
60–70	2–7 hrs.	2–40 hrs.
70–80	3–12 hrs.	3 hrs.–?

The greatest change in survival time occurs as the water temperature drops below 50 degrees.

Swimming in cold water increases the flow of water past the body, pumping heat out of the clothing so that heat production is outpaced by heat loss. If there is no prospect of getting out of the water immediately, survival time will be longer if one does not swim but relies on a life jacket for flotation. Better still, assume the HELP position (Heat Escape Lessening Position) in which the knees are tucked close to the chest. This allows one to retain body heat longer. It is, therefore, imperative that a life jacket with adequate flotation be worn. Swim only if there is danger downstream.

In recent years a number of new materials have been developed that make cold weather paddling more comfortable and certainly safer. Materials such as polypropylene, pile, and fleece tend to wick wetness away from the body and dry very quickly. Wool has the ability to provide warmth when wet, but the newer materials do it better. Worn under a paddling jacket and pants, they can be very effective. For the decked boater who is more likely to get wet, a wet or dry suit is highly recommended. Also, a polypro or wool cap can help tremendously because a great deal of body heat is lost through an unprotected head or neck.

Dry clothing should definitely be carried in a waterproof bag on all winter trips and changed into if one gets wet. Quite often you must insist that the victim change clothing and render assistance in changing because of his lack of coordination. The victim more than likely will be totally unaware of his poor reactions.

Symptoms of exposure occur generally as follows: uncontrollable shivering; vague, slow, slurred speech; memory lapses; slowing of reactions, fumbling hands, and apparent exhaustion. Unconsciousness will follow and then death. The mental effects will be similar to those observed in states of extreme fatigue.

In cases of extreme exposure, build a fire and give the victim a warm drink, if he is able to swallow; strip him and put him into a sleeping bag with another person who is also stripped. Remember that the victim must be warmed from an outside heat source since he cannot generate his own body heat. Do not give the victim any form of alcohol.

Paddler Information

The most widely publicized paddler self-evaluation was created by the Keel-Haulers Canoe Club of Ohio. Their system brings the problem of matching paddlers with rivers into perspective but seems to overemphasize non-paddling skills. A canoe clinic student who is athletically inclined but almost totally without paddling skill once achieved a rating of 15 points using the Keel-Haulers system. His rating, based almost exclusively on general fitness and strength, incorrectly implied that he was capable of handling many Class II and Class III rivers. A second problem evident in the system is the lack of depth in skill category descriptions. Finally, confusion exists in several rating areas as to whether the evaluation applies to open canoes, decked canoes, or both.

To remedy these perceived shortcomings and to bring added objectivity to paddler self-evaluation, Bob Sehlinger, co-author of this book, has refined the paddler rating system. Admittedly the refined system is more complex and exhaustive, but not more so than warranted by the situation.

Rating the Paddler

Instructions: All items, except the first, carry points that may be added to obtain an overall rating. All items except "Rolling Ability" apply to both open and decked boats. Rate open and decked boat skills separately.

---

1. Prerequisite Skills. Before paddling on moving current, the paddler should:

   a. Have some swimming ability.

b. Be able to paddle instinctively on nonmoving water (lake). This presumes knowledge of basic strokes.

c. Be able to guide and control the canoe from either side without changing paddling sides.

d. Be able to guide and control the canoe (or kayak) while paddling backwards.

e. Be able to move the canoe (or kayak) laterally.

f. Understand the limitations of the boat.

g. Be practiced in "wet exit" if in a decked boat.

2. Equipment. Award points on the suitability of your equipment to whitewater. Whether you own, borrow, or rent the equipment makes no difference. Do not award points for both open canoe and decked boat.

Open Canoe

0 Points: Any canoe less than 15 feet for tandem; any canoe less than 14 feet for solo.

1 Point: Canoe with moderate rocker, full depth, and recurved bow; should be ≥ 15 feet in length for tandem and ≥ 14 feet in length for solo and have bow and stern painters.

2 Points: Whitewater canoe. Strong rocker design, full bow with recurve, full depth amidships, no keel; meets or exceeds minimum length requirements as described under "1 Point"; made of hand-laid fiberglass, Kevlar, Marlex, or ABS Royalex; has bow and stern painters. Canoe as described under "1 Point" but with extra flotation.

3 Points: Canoe as described under "2 Points" but with extra flotation.

Decked Boat

0 Points: Any decked boat lacking full flotation, spray skirt, or foot braces.

1 Point: Any fully equipped, decked boat with a wooden frame.

2 Points: Decked boat with full flotation, spray skirt and foot braces; has grab loops; made of any modern composite material.

3 Points: Decked boat with foam wall reinforcement and split flotation; Neoprene spray skirt; boat has knee braces, foot braces, and grab loops.

3. Experience. Compute the following to determine preliminary points, then convert the preliminary points to final points according to the conversion table.

Number of days spent each year paddling:

Class I rivers	x	1	____
Class II rivers	x	2	____
Class III rivers	x	3	____
Class IV rivers	x	4	____
Class V rivers	x	5	____
Preliminary Subtotal			____
Number of years paddling experience	+		____
Total Preliminary Points			____

Conversion Table

Preliminary Points	Final Points
0–20	0
21–60	1
61–100	2
101–200	3
201–300	4
301–up	5

Note: This is the only evaluation item where it is possible to accrue more than 3 points.

---

4. Swimming

0 Points: Cannot swim.
1 Point: Weak swimmer.
2 Points: Average swimmer.
3 Points: Strong swimmer (competition level or skin diver).

---

5. Stamina

0 Points: Cannot run mile in less than 10 minutes.
1 Point: Can run a mile in 7 to 10 minutes.
2 Points: Can run a mile in less than 7 minutes.

---

6. Upper Body Strength

0 Points: Cannot do 15 push-ups.
1 Point: Can do 16 to 25 push-ups.
2 Points: Can do more than 25 push-ups.

---

7. Boat Control

0 Points: Can keep boat fairly straight.
1 Point: Can maneuver in moving water; can avoid big obstacles.
2 Points: Can maneuver in heavy water; knows how to work with the current.

3 Points: Finesse in boat placement in all types of water; uses current to maximum advantage.

8. Aggressiveness
0 Points: Does not play or work river at all.
1 Point: Timid; plays a little on familiar streams.
2 Points: Plays a lot; works most rivers hard.
3 Points: Plays in heavy water with grace and confidence.

9. Eddy Turns
0 Points: Has difficulty making eddy turns from moderate current.
1 Point: Can make eddy turns in either direction from moderate current; can enter moderate current from eddy.
2 Points: Can catch medium eddies in either direction from heavy current; can enter very swift current from eddy.
3 Points: Can catch small eddies in heavy current.

10. Ferrying
0 Points: Cannot ferry.
1 Point: Can ferry upstream and downstream in moderate current.
2 Points: Can ferry upstream in heavy current; can ferry downstream in moderate current.
3 Points: Can ferry upstream and downstream in heavy current.

11. Water Reading
0 Points: Often in error.
1 Point: Can plan route in short rapid with several well spaced obstacles.
2 Points: Can confidently run lead through continuous Class II; can predict the effects of waves and holes on boat.
3 Points: Can confidently run lead in continuous Class III; has knowledge to predict and handle the effects of reversals, side currents, and turning drops.

12. Judgment
0 Points: Often in error.
1 Point: Has average ability to analyze difficulty of rapids.
2 Points: Has good ability to analyze difficulty of rapids and make independent judgments as to which should not be run.
3 Points: Has the ability to assist fellow paddlers in evaluating the difficulty of rapids; can explain subtleties to paddlers with less experience.

13. Bracing
0 Points: Has difficulty bracing in Class II water.

1 Point: Can correctly execute bracing strokes in Class II water.

2 Points: Can correctly brace in intermittent whitewater with medium waves and vertical drops of 3 feet or less.

3 Points: Can brace effectively in continuous whitewater with large waves and large vertical drops (4 feet and up).

---

14. Rescue Ability

0 Points: Self-rescue in flatwater.

1 Point: Self-rescue in mild whitewater.

2 Points: Self-rescue in Class III: can assist others in mild whitewater.

3 Points: Can assist others in heavy whitewater.

---

15. Rolling Ability

0 Points: Can only roll in pool.

1 Point: Can roll 3 out of 4 times in moving current.

2 Points: Can roll 3 out of 4 times in Class II whitewater.

3 Points: Can roll 4 out of 5 times in Class III and IV whitewater.

Knowing Your Rights on the River

The definition of a "navigable" stream is open to discussion. The term is not clear and its interpretation has sparked controversy all across the country. In Kentucky, a navigable stream is one that can support either commercial or recreational boating. That covers a lot of water—the commercial classification meaning specifically barge traffic, the recreational aspect connoting powerboats, canoes, kayaks, rafts, houseboats, and so on. It's a broad, debatable term especially in the eyes of the mining industry, which cannot pollute navigable waters without being fined. Attempts have been made in the past to protect all waterways from flagrant pollution, but the measure met with defeat in the state legislature due to heavy opposition from mining lobbyists.

The paddler's right to run rivers, all of which are "in the public domain," is guaranteed in Kentucky statutes. Landowners' rights to prohibit trespassing on their land along creeks, if they so desire, are also guaranteed. Therefore, access to rivers must be secured at highway rights-of-way or on publicly owned lands if permission to cross privately owned lands cannot be secured. In granting you access to a river, landowners are extending a privilege to you as they extend such to hunters who stop by their doors and seek permission to shoot doves in their cornfields. Don't betray landowners' trust if they extend to you the privilege to camp or launch canoes or kayaks from their riverbanks. Don't litter, drive through newly planted fields, or forget to close gates. Tenure of land, landholding, and the right to do with it what you want, is serious business to landowners. Some farmers can't accept the concept of "land stewardship" ascribed to by many city paddlers today. They don't feel any compulsion or responsibility toward the paddling community and their pursuit of legal rights. In some cases they might even resent people driving hundreds of miles for the pleasure of floating down a river. They may even feel that they "own" the river you want to paddle.

On the other hand, it may be that the landowner you seek permission from is intrigued with paddling and will be quite friendly and approachable. Value this friendship and don't give cause to deny you access to the river at some time in the future.

Paddlers are trespassing when they portage, camp, or even stop for a lunch break, if they disembark from their boats on the water. If you are approached by a landowner when trespassing, by all means be cordial and understanding and explain your predicament (in the case of a portage or lunch break). Never knowingly camp on private land without permission. If you do encounter a perturbed landowner, don't panic. Keep cool and be respectful.

Landowners certainly have the right to keep you off their land, and the law will side with them unless they inflict harm upon you, in which case they may be both civilly or criminally liable. If you threaten a landowner verbally, and physically move toward him or her with apparent will to do harm, he or she has all the rights of self-defense and can protect himself or herself in accordance with the perceived danger that you impose. Likewise, if the landowner points a gun at you, fires warning shots, assaults, injures, or wounds you or a boater in your group, you are certainly in the right to protect yourself. The landowner has no right to detain you as if holding you for the sheriff. If you fear for your own life at the hands of the landowner, you do have the right to protect yourself.

The confrontations between belligerent paddlers and cantankerous landowners are to be avoided, that's for sure. Although the happenstance of such a meeting may be rare, paddlers nonetheless should know their rights, and the rights of landowners. Judges don't like trespassers any more than they like landowners who shoot trespassers.

Environmental Concerns

Water quality is an ever-important issue as Kentucky becomes more populated. Presenting a set of environmental guidelines for all paddlers sounds like preaching, but with the number of persons using our creeks and rivers today, it is indeed a valid point.

Many of the streams listed in this guide flow through national parks and forests, state owned forests and wildlife management areas, and privately owned lands that in some cases are superior in quality and aesthetics to lands under public ownership. It is the paddling community's responsibility to uphold the integrity of these lands and their rivers by exercising environmentally sound guidelines. Litter, fire scars, pollution from human excrement and cutting live trees is unsightly and affects the land in a way that threatens to ruin the outdoor experience for everyone.

Keep in mind that litter and liquid pollutants often ends up in streams by non-paddlers. That piece of trash by the highway, or oil from an auto leak flows into a stream during a storm and enters the watershed. It is our job to keep our waterways clean no matter where we are. While on the river, paddlers should pack out everything they packed in: all paper litter and such non-biodegradable items as cartons, foil, plastic jugs, and cans. Help keep our waterways clean for those who follow. If you are canoe camping, leave your campsite in better shape than you found it. If you must build a fire, build it at an established site, and when you leave, dismantle rock fireplaces, thoroughly drown all flames and hot coals, and scatter the ashes. Never cut live trees for firewood. Use biodegradable soap and dump all dishwater at least 100 feet away from watercourses.

Using This Guide

First, an **overview description** of the river is given, followed by detail of **maps** that can be used for that particular section of river. Topographic maps are listed in the order in which the river flows. Unless otherwise noted as above, all maps are located on the Kentucky Index of the United States Geological Survey. If there is not a local source for maps they can be ordered on the Web at www.topozone.com. Next, the **specific section of the river** is spelled out. The **shuttle** portion lists the exact take-out and put-in with directions to a particular highway or secondary road bridge. The **gauge** section tells readers exactly which gauges are needed to determine river runnability.

Beside the narrative are headings for each river, listing the following data: river difficulty, river gauge, water level, velocity, river gradient, and scenery. **River difficulty** classification is adapted from the system used by American Whitewater. Difficulty is rated Class I–VI. For detailed information on the rating system, refer to the Rating River Difficulty section below. **Gauge** indicates whether the gauge of the river is visual, phone, or Web. If visual, you literally have to look at the river to determine whether it is runnable or not. Phone indicates you can call a number to find out if it is runnable. and Web means you can look on the Internet to find out whether it can be floated. **Level** indicates the flow rates at which a particular river can be run. Each section of river has its own personality when it comes to "too high" or "too low." A useful range is indicated by a comfortable minimum and a reasonable maximum flow rate. Rivers can be run at much higher levels by experts who know them well and at significantly lower levels by determined rock bashers who do not mind wading and lifting over shallow places. Where we do not have a specific figure we list the level as N/A, meaning not available.

Government agencies like the United States Geological Survey (USGS) measure river flows at gauging stations throughout the country. This information is collected and recorded hourly. You will find pertinent Web sites and phone numbers listed in the discussion of river gauges below. You will also encounter "paddlers gauges" painted on bridge piers and rocks. Although not reported on Web sites and such, they remain in use. **Velocity** is the speed of the current, on the average, in nonflood conditions. It can vary incredibly from section to section on a given stream depending on the steam's width, volume, and gradient at any point along its length. Velocity is a partial indicator on how much reaction time you might have on a certain river. **Gradient** is the average drop of the river in feet per mile. If parts of the river drop at a value significantly different from the average, we indicate this by parentheses. For example, 7 means that while the river drops at an average rate of 7 feet per mile. Remember: the difficulty of a river's rapids is not determined by gradient alone. Some rivers drop evenly over continuous rapids of roughly the same difficulty. Others alternate between long pools and drops that are steeper than the gradient would indicate. Waterfalls are an extreme example of this. Geological peculiarities, such as huge boulders, high ledges, and gorges must also be considered. The accompanying river descriptions will give some insight. **Scenery** is ranked on an A to D scale, A—remote wilderness areas with little sign of civilization, B—more settled, but still beautiful pastoral countryside, C—lots of development (cities or industry), D—pollution, strip mines, tipples, slag-heaps, rundown buildings, and other forms of landscape abuse.

The quality of the scenery along a river can change. For example, the Green River within Mammoth Cave National Park considered B, even A at times, but becomes C on its lower reaches where barges are common. However, cities and manufactured settings are not necessarily eyesores.

Finally, maps accompanying each river included in this guide-book. These maps will aid paddlers in finding their way but are no substitute for detailed USGS topographic maps, county maps or map books such as that put out by DeLorme.

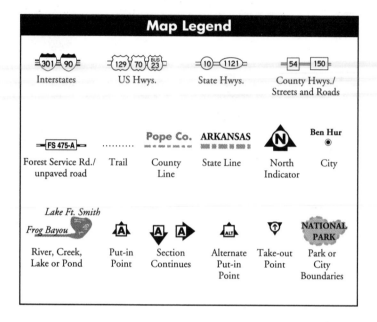

Map Legend

301 **90** — Interstates	**129** **70** **BUS 23** — US Hwys.	**10** **1121** — State Hwys.	**54** **150** — County Hwys./ Streets and Roads

FS 475-A — Forest Service Rd./ unpaved road

·········· Trail

Pope Co. — County Line

ARKANSAS — State Line

N — North Indicator

Ben Hur ● — City

Lake Ft. Smith
Frog Bayou — River, Creek, Lake or Pond

A — Put-in Point

A **A** — Section Continues

A ALT — Alternate Put-in Point

— Take-out Point

NATIONAL PARK — Park or City Boundaries

part**One**

RUSSELL FORK

Flowing out of Virginia and joined by the Pound River, the Russell Fork cuts a 1,600-foot gorge in the lonely Pine Ridge Mountains, forming what is referred to as the Great Breaks of the Pine Ridge. This incredible chasm with giant vertical walls and pounding whitewater bisects the Kentucky–Virginia border for several miles before plunging out of the mountains near Elkhorn City, Kentucky.

Before the 1990s, this river was seldom run but has since become a paddling mecca for whitewater enthusiasts from Kentucky, Virginia, and beyond, especially during the fall whitewater releases from the Flannagan Dam. The dammed Pound River joins the free-flowing Russell Fork at Bartlick, Virgina. From here, the river punches into a rugged gorge from the Garden Hole through The Breaks into Kentucky. The rapids ease up a bit beyond old Potters Ford, now known as Ratliff Hole, the first take-out beyond the gorge, before flowing into Elkhorn City.

MAPS: Elkhorn City, KY; Dickenson, VA (USGS)

BARTLICK BRIDGE TO GARDEN HOLE

class	II–III+
gauge	Web
level	Min. 400
	Max. 1500
	(cfs)
velocity	2.6–5.0+
	(mph)
gradient	28 (fpm)
scenery	A

DESCRIPTION: With the exception of fall water releases from Flannagan Dam, Bartlick Bridge is the most commonly used upper access. This section becomes Class IV when the water is above 1,500 cfs. At normal water levels, this is a good intermediate run. In fall, paddlers start below Flannagan Dam, which adds 1.5 miles of water to the run. The put-in is in Virginia on the Pound River, below the dam, with easy Class II water on down to the confluence with the Russell Fork. Below the confluence, the gradient begins to increase, and the river broadens slightly to accommodate the additional volume. As canyon walls begin to rise on both sides, Garden Hole access can be seen near the river's edge on the right. For anyone beginning to feel a little overwhelmed, this is the last chance to stop before entering the gorge.

GAUGE: The gauge used for Russell Fork is a combination of two USGS gauges: Russell Fork at Haysi, VA, and Pound River below Flannagan Dam near Haysi, VA. Add the two and use the number to determine floatability. Minimum level is 400 cfs, maximum level is 1,500 cfs.

Points	River Miles	Shuttle Miles
A—B	4.67	11.78
B—C	3.78	6.22
C—D	1.89	2.0
D—E	0.6	0.52

THE GORGE, GARDEN HOLE TO RATLIFF HOLE OR FORD

class	IV–V+
gauge	Web
level	Min. 125
	Max. 1,400
	(cfs)
velocity	2.6–5.0+
	(mph)
gradient	140, with
	sections up
	to 190 (fpm)
scenery	A+

DESCRIPTION: At the Garden Hole, the drop increases markedly, and steep sandstone walls rise on both sides. The Russell Fork now pounds its way along a giant semicircular loop at the base of the mountain. Here, hidden by the shadows of the gorge, is a hellish continuum of thundering vertical drops and foam-blasted boulder gardens, where the river gradient reaches 190 feet per mile!

Many of the rapids in this section, including the consecutive 5-, 8-, and 9-foot vertical drops of Triple Drop; the awesome El Horrendo with drops of 10 and 15 feet, spaced only a boat length apart; and the boulder-strewn S-turn at Red Cliff had never been run before October 1976. This section is now run regularly but is still a solid Class V+. Needless to say, this section is for experts in top condition with bulletproof rolls.

Although scouting is not difficult, and portage routes around the major rapids are available, the rapids are intensely complex, technical, violent, and continuous. An upset in one of the milder rapids (Class III–IV) could lead to a nightmare swim through a Class V+ run. Dangers on this run, other than the obvious, include two long railroad tunnels on the left ridge that some paddlers risk walking through to facilitate scouting.

Beyond the loop, the river turns north and heads toward Elkhorn City, passing Ratliff Hole, the take-out for the gorge. Formerly known as Potters Ford, Ratliff Hole has a steep road to tackle, but river access is excellent. This locale is a gathering spot for paddling enthusiasts, who trade tales of taming the now-famed whitewater that is Russell Fork.

GAUGE: The gauge used for Russell Fork is a combination of two USGS gauges: Russell Fork at Haysi, VA, and Pound River below Flannagan Dam near Haysi, VA. Add the two and use the number to determine floatability. Minimum level is 125 cfs, maximum level is 1,400 cfs.

RATLIFF HOLE TO ELKHORN CITY

class	II–III
gauge	Web
level	Min. 200 Max. 5,000 (cfs)
velocity	2.6–5.0+ (mph)
gradient	20 (fpm)
scenery	A

DESCRIPTION: This section starts at Ratliff Hole, formerly known as Potters Ford. This is the take-out for the gorge section of the Russell Fork. Although primarily Class II rapids, the run does have one Class III. It is not normally run in open canoes but is used for training in play boats and rafts.

GAUGE: The gauge used for Russell Fork is a combination of two USGS gauges, Russell Fork at Haysi, VA, combined with Pound River below Flannagan Dam near Haysi, VA. Add the two together and use the number to determine floatability. Minimum level is 200 cfs, maximum level is 5000 cfs. This combined gauge is posted on the American Whitewater Association Web site.

LEVISA FORK OF THE BIG SANDY RIVER

The Levisa Fork flows out of Virginia into Pike County in southeastern Kentucky, where it is impounded to form Fishtrap Lake. Below the lake, the Levisa Fork makes up one of the major drainages of eastern Kentucky as it flows through Floyd, Johnson, and Lawrence counties before coming together with the Tug Fork to form the Big Sandy River. Runnable almost all year below the dam at Fishtrap Lake to its confluence with the Tug Fork, the Levisa Fork is big—averaging 80 to 110 feet in width. Civilization is continuous along the Levisa Fork, with a highway paralleling the stream on one side and a railroad on the other. Additionally, the Levisa Fork runs through the sizable communities of Pikeville, Paintsville, Prestonsburg, and Louisa. Amazingly, despite the overwhelming human presence, the Levisa Fork is not a total loss as a canoeing stream. Sunk between deep banks that hide the bustle of civilization, the stream itself is tree-lined and not at all unpleasant. Access is plentiful along its entire length and the river is free of powerboat traffic, except for a small stretch in Lawrence County. Tall hills and bluffs (some man-made) make for pleasant viewing. The Levisa Fork's level of difficulty is Class I with occasional small shoals and rapids (Class I+). Dangers to navigation are limited to deadfalls (which are easily avoided), a man-made rapid below Louisa, and several low-water bridges. Difficulties also include a mud bottom and banks of soft sand that can easily swallow paddlers up to their waist if they step in the wrong place when putting in or taking out.

MAPS: Millard, Pikeville, Broadbottom, Harold, Lancer, Prestonsburg, Paintsville, Offutt, Richardson, Milo, Louisa (USGS)

FISHTRAP LAKE DAM TO BANNER OR TO POINT G

DESCRIPTION: The river often flows clear from below Fishtrap Dam. It is 8 miles from the dam to KY 122, 13 miles from KY 122 to the north side of Pikeville, and 21 miles farther to Banner.

GAUGE: The USGS gauge is Levisa Fork at Pikeville. The minimum reading should be 400.

class	I (II)
gauge	Web
level	Min. 400 Max. flood (cfs)
velocity	2.6–5.0 (mph)
gradient	1.5 (fpm)
scenery	C

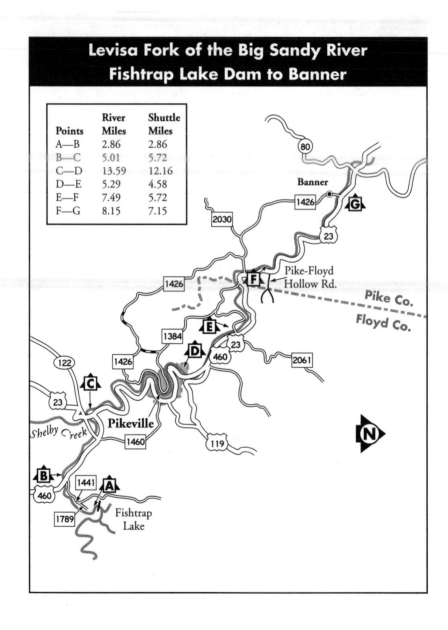

Levisa Fork of the Big Sandy River
Fishtrap Lake Dam to Banner

Points	River Miles	Shuttle Miles
A—B	2.86	2.86
B—C	5.01	5.72
C—D	13.59	12.16
D—E	5.29	4.58
E—F	7.49	5.72
F—G	8.15	7.15

BANNER TO PAINTSVILLE

DESCRIPTION: The average width of the river here is 80 to 100 feet. It is 7 miles from Banner to the junction of KY 1428 and KY 194, and 13.5 miles farther to Auxier and the mouth of Johns Creek. It is 11 miles from Auxier to Paintsville.

class	I (II)
gauge	Web
level	Min. 400 Max. flood (cfs)
velocity	2.6–5.0 (mph)
gradient	1.2 (fpm)
scenery	C

Levisa Fork of the Big Sandy River
Banner to Paintsville

Points	River Miles	Shuttle Miles
G—H	7.15	5.58
H—I	13.4	11.6
I—J	10.73	10.01

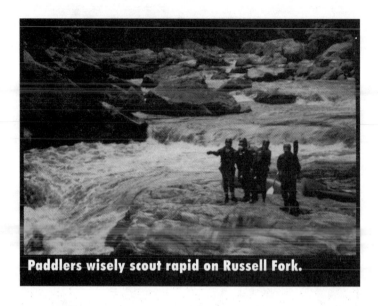

Paddlers wisely scout rapid on Russell Fork.

GAUGE: The USGS gauge is Levisa Fork at Paintsville. The minimum reading should be 400.

PAINTSVILLE TO LOUISA

class	I (II)
gauge	Web
level	Min. 400 Max. flood (cfs)
velocity	2.6–5.0 (mph)
gradient	1.0 (fpm)
scenery	C

DESCRIPTION: This section of river ranges from 80 to 110 feet wide. KY 581 offers nearly continuous scouting opportunities. It is 12 miles from Paintsville to the next access on KY 581, and 18 miles farther to the US 23 access near KY 1760. It is 17.5 miles from the US 23/KY 1760 access to Louisa.

GAUGE: The USGS gauge is Levisa Fork at Paintsville. The minimum reading should be 400.

Levisa Fork of the Big Sandy River
Paintsville to Louisa

Points	River Miles	Shuttle Miles
J—K	10.9	7.87
K—L	12.87	11.44
L—M	5.43	5.72
M—N	4.86	4.29
N—O	9.3	9.58
O—P	3.43	5.72

Big Sandy River

Dangerous man-made rapids

Louisa

Lawrence Co.
Johnson Co.

Paintville

JOHNS CREEK

Johns Creek flows northwest out of Pike County into Dewey Lake and from there through Floyd County to empty into the Levisa Fork of the Big Sandy River south of Paintsville. Scenery on both sections consists of wooded hillsides and sandy banks with dense scrub vegetation.

MAPS: Prestonsburg (USGS)

KY 194 TO DEWEY LAKE

class	I
gauge	Web
level	Min. 100 Max. flood (cfs)
velocity	2.6–5.0 (mph)
gradient	1.0 (fpm)
scenery	C

DESCRIPTION: The upper section from KY 194 to Dewey Lake can be run all year. Occasional logs border one side or another of the stream, which averages 20–30 feet wide above Dewey Lake. The upper section is almost devoid of current as a rule but is a passable canoe-camping run when combined with portions of Dewey Lake, a normally clear impoundment. Dewey Lake has multiple access points, including roadside pull-offs. KY 194 runs along upper Johns Creek, offering scouting opportunities. Access to the upper section is plentiful and good.

GAUGE: The USGS gauge is Johns Creek near Meta, KY. The minimum reading should be 100 cfs.

Johns Creek

Points	River Miles	Shuttle Miles
A—B	13.0	22.0

LITTLE SANDY RIVER

The Little Sandy River is born in southern Elliott County and flows northeast to the Ohio River through Carter and Greenup Counties.

MAPS: Sandy Hook, Isonville, Bruin, Willard, Grayson, Old-town, Argillite, Greenup (USGS)

SANDY HOOK TO GRAYSON LAKE

class	I–II
gauge	Visual
level	Min. 140 Max. flood (cfs)
velocity	2.6–5.0 (mph)
gradient	4.6 (fpm)
scenery	A+

DESCRIPTION: From Sandy Hook to the Dehart Road Bridge above Grayson Lake, the stream is runnable from January through April and following heavy rains at any time of year. This section is beautiful beyond belief, with exposed rock bluffs and overhangs and a luxurious forest of both evergreens and hardwoods. Interspaced along the river are flat terraces carpeted with lush bluegrass, perfect for camping. The Little Sandy flows over a bed of gravel and mud in this upper gorge section with frequent sandbars and small Class I+ rapids to make paddling interesting. The river's width is from 20 to 35 feet on average. Navigational hazards are primarily deadfalls washed into the gorge from above Sandy Hook.

From the KY 7 bridge, near its junction with KY 706, downstream into Grayson Lake, the Little Sandy can be run all year thanks to the water backup from the lake pool. This section also runs through a gorge and is extremely scenic, with small waterfalls visible at adjoining feeder streams. Obviously, due to the backwash, the stream is wider here (75–80 feet) and there is no current. Access is good, and many take-outs are available according to how far into the lake you wish to paddle. This section is excellent for canoe camping and there are no navigational hazards.

It is 11 miles from Sandy Hook to the KY 7 bridge near KY 706 and 15.5 miles farther to the Clifty Creek embayment access on Grayson Lake.

ABOUT THE SHUTTLE: To reach the lower access from Exit 172 on I-64, take KY 1/7 South. Stay with KY 7 over Grayson Lake Dam. Turn left just before the Clifty Creek embayment and a boat ramp on the right. If you reach South Clifty Access for the

Grayson Lake Wildlife Management Area, you have gone a half-mile too far and over the Clifty Creek embayment.

GAUGE: The nonlake section of the Little Sandy is simply a look-and-see proposition from January through April and following heavy rains the rest of the year.

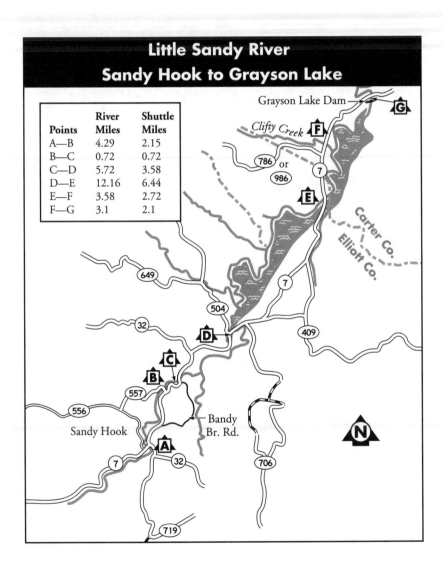

Little Sandy River
Sandy Hook to Grayson Lake

Points	River Miles	Shuttle Miles
A—B	4.29	2.15
B—C	0.72	0.72
C—D	5.72	3.58
D—E	12.16	6.44
E—F	3.58	2.72
F—G	3.1	2.1

class	I–II
gauge	Web
level	Min. 150
	Max. flood
	(cfs)
velocity	2.6–5.0
	(mph)
gradient	1.6 (fpm)
scenery	A to B–

GRAYSON LAKE DAM TO OHIO RIVER

DESCRIPTION: The Little Sandy continues to be extraordinary from the tailwater of the dam (off KY 7 in Carter County) to the intersection of the new KY 7 bridge near Leon. Small and intimate, once again the river averages 25–40 feet in width and flows beneath steep rock walls and overhangs on the west and forest (with some cultivated land) on the east. This section can be combined with a loop of the Jenny Wiley Trail, which runs along the river, starting at the base of the dam. The run ends with a small Class II rapid at the KY 7 bridge. Access is good, and navigational dangers are limited to an occasional deadfall. Runnable most of the year, the water level is dependent on releases from the dam.

Downstream of the new KY 7 bridge toward Grayson, the river flows through a wide valley, pastoral in setting but with increased human habitation. Although not nearly as scenic as the upstream sections, the river continues to make for pleasant paddling. Departing the Grayson Plain, the Little Sandy River proceeds northeast through gently rolling farmland toward the Ohio River. Increasing to 40–50 feet in width and running over a mud bottom with 9–16-feet mud banks, the river stays substantially the same through northern Carter County and all of Greenup County. Access is good. Navigational dangers are minimal and are once again limited primarily to deadfalls. A special point of interest in Greenup County is a historic covered bridge spanning the stream near Oldtown.

ABOUT THE SHUTTLE: To reach the access below Grayson Lake Dam from Exit 172, keep south on KY 1/7. Stay with KY 7, cross Grayson Lake Dam, and turn right in the U.S. Army Corps of Engineers recreation area, toward shelter #4. The put-in is near shelter #4.

GAUGE: The USGS gauge is Little Sandy River at Grayson, KY. The minimum reading should be 150 cfs.

Grayson Lake Dam to Ohio River

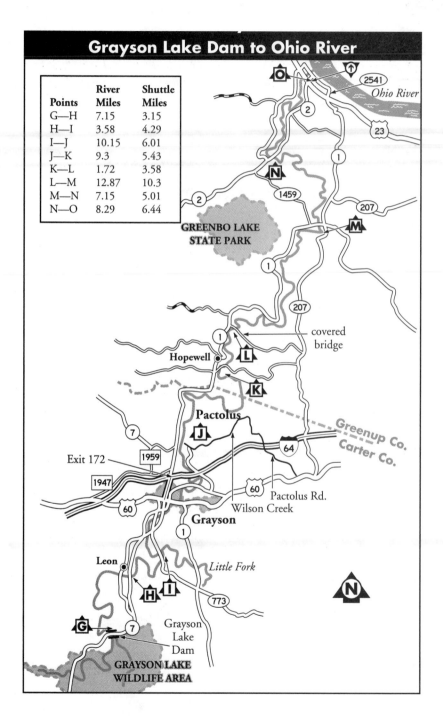

Points	River Miles	Shuttle Miles
G—H	7.15	3.15
H—I	3.58	4.29
I—J	10.15	6.01
J—K	9.3	5.43
K—L	1.72	3.58
L—M	12.87	10.3
M—N	7.15	5.01
N—O	8.29	6.44

Ohio River

GREENBO LAKE STATE PARK

covered bridge

Hopewell

Pactolus

Greenup Co.
Carter Co.

Exit 172

Pactolus Rd.
Wilson Creek

Grayson

Leon   *Little Fork*

Grayson Lake Dam

GRAYSON LAKE WILDLIFE AREA

TYGARTS CREEK

Originating in southwestern Carter County, Tygarts Creek flows northeast through Carter and Greenup Counties to empty into the Ohio River across the river from Portsmouth, Ohio. The best paddling section, however, runs from Olive Hill to Carter Caves State Park.

MAPS: Olive Hill, Grahn, Tygarts Valley (USGS)

OLIVE HILL TO CARTER CAVES STATE PARK

class	I–II
gauge	Web and visual
level	Min. 300 Max. flood (cfs)
velocity	2.6–5.0 (mph)
gradient	2.0 (fpm)
scenery	A

DESCRIPTION: From Olive Hill to the KY 182 bridge near Carter Caves State Resort Park, this creek flows through a deep, secluded gorge with evergreen- and hardwood-topped bluffs and some borderline Class II rapids. Runnable in late winter through early spring and after heavy rains, this section abounds in wildlife. Throughout the gorge, Tygarts Creek is extremely narrow (15–25 feet) and swiftly flows over a rock, sand, and gravel bottom. Navigational dangers include deadfalls, logjams, and an undercut rock on the left shortly after passing under the I-64 bridge.

From the KY 182 bridge downstream, Tygarts Creek continues to flow through a gorge for an additional 5 miles before descending into the valley south of Iron Hill. Although the beginning of this section is very scenic, the final several miles are rather lackluster (as is the remainder of the creek as it flows northeast toward the Ohio). Between Iron Hill and its mouth, Tygarts Creek can be run from November to mid-June but it is not particularly appealing. The river's width here is 30–45 feet with steep banks of mud. Vegetation at riverside is essentially scrub weeds, and trees are conspicuously absent. Surrounding terrain is rolling farmland with some cultivation of the flattened floodplains adjoining the stream. Deadfalls and logjams are common, as are some of the less aesthetic effects of lateral erosion. One bright spot in this section, however, is a covered bridge half a mile south of the Plum Fork church in Greenup County. Access from Iron Hill to the Ohio River is poor.

GAUGE: The USGS gauge, Tygarts Creek near Greenup, KY, is downstream of the preferred section of the Tygarts but can be used as an aid. A reading of 300 cfs or higher is best to float the upper section. However, a visual inspection will confirm floatability of the creek.

Tygarts Creek

Points	River Miles	Shuttle Miles
A—B	12.16	7.15

CENTER CAVES STATE PARK

Olive Hill

N

part**Two**

THE LICKING RIVER AND ITS TRIBUTARIES

NORTH FORK OF THE LICKING RIVER

Flowing from east to west, the North Fork of the Licking River drains portions of Lewis, Fleming, Mason, Bracken, and Robertson Counties before joining the Middle Fork of the Licking River southeast of Falmouth. Running over a mud and limestone bottom through hilly grazing land, the North Fork often diverts around small islands of scrub vegetation.

MAPS: Orangeburg, Mays Lick, Sardis, Mount Olivet, Claysville (USGS)

LEWISBURG TO RILEY MILL BRIDGE

class	I
gauge	Web
level	Min. 200
	Max. flood
	(cfs)
velocity	2.6–5.0
	(mph)
gradient	2.65 (fpm)
scenery	C

DESCRIPTION: The North Fork can be canoed west of Lewisburg in Mason County from November through early June but is not particularly appealing. The entire North Fork is a Class I stream with deadfalls and logjams posing the major hazards to navigation. There are numerous access points, making trips of varied lengths possible.

GAUGE: The USGS gauge is North Fork Licking River at Mt. Olivet. The minimum reading should be 200 cfs.

North Fork of the Licking River

Points	River Miles	Shuttle Miles
A—B	3.43	2.86
B—C	7.01	4.58
C—D	4.29	6.44
D—E	6.58	8.58
E—F	5.01	4.15
F—G	4.58	8.15
G—H	7.87	5.72
H—I	2.15	2.5
I—J	8.37	9.15
J—K	4.43	0.72

MIDDLE FORK OF THE LICKING RIVER

The Middle Fork of the Licking River originates in southern Magof-fin County and flows northwest, draining portions of Morgan (where the river empties into Cave Run Lake), Menifee, Rowan, Bath, Fleming, Nicholas, Robertson, Harrison, and Pendleton Counties. From the KY 32 bridge to its confluence with the North and South Forks, the river is runnable all year long.

The Middle Fork of the Licking River runs through hilly farm-land and woodlands. Flowing over a bottom of sand and mud with mud banks of varying steepness, the stream is generally lined with hardwood and scrub vegetation. Sandbars and islands of grass and scrub vegetation are common all along its length (even at relatively high water), and deadfalls are common. Many access points are on private property where permission must be obtained to put in or take out. All runs from the dam to the confluence with North Fork are Class I, but the current can be extremely swift and forceful in the spring. As it flows north, the Middle Fork broadens from 25 feet at the tailwater of the dam to 60 feet in the Blue Licks area to 95–110 feet at its confluence with the South Fork in Falmouth.

MAPS: Bangor, Salt Lick, Farmers, Colfax, Hillsboro, Sherburne, Moorefield, Cowan, Piqua, Shady Nook, Claysville, Berlin, Falmouth (USGS)

TAILWATER OF CAVE RUN DAM TO KY 32

class	I
gauge	Phone
level	Min. 120 Max. flood (cfs)
velocity	2.6–5.0 (mph)
gradient	1.2 (fpm)
scenery	C+

DESCRIPTION: From its origin to Cave Run Lake, the Middle Fork is littered, jammed, and generally too small to canoe. From the tailwater of the dam downstream to the KY 32 bridge near Myers, the Middle Fork is runnable from mid-October to early June, subject to water releases from the dam. The river passes under a covered bridge on KY 11. It is 4 miles from the tailwater of the dam to US 60, 17 miles to the KY 211 bridge, and 34 miles farther to the covered bridge. The Clay Wildlife Management Area, on the west bank below KY 57 bridge, affords the opportunity for canoe-camping.

GAUGE: Call the U.S. Army Corps of Engineers at (606) 784-9709 to receive water release schedule from Cave Run Lake Dam. The minimum release needs to be 120 cfs.

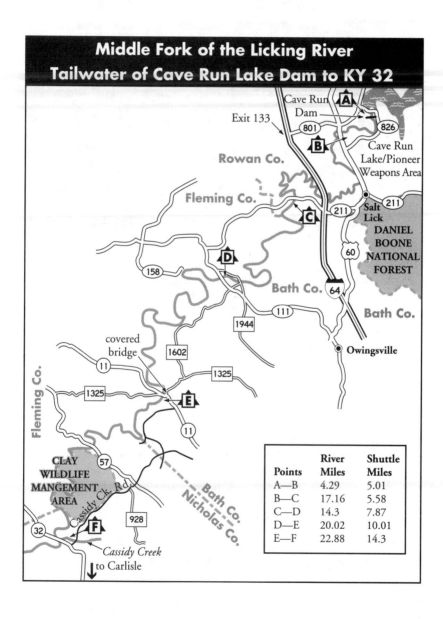

Middle Fork of the Licking River
Tailwater of Cave Run Lake Dam to KY 32

Points	River Miles	Shuttle Miles
A—B	4.29	5.01
B—C	17.16	5.58
C—D	14.3	7.87
D—E	20.02	10.01
E—F	22.88	14.3

KY 32 TO CLAYSVILLE

class	I
gauge	Phone
level	Min. 120
	Max. flood
	(cfs)
velocity	2.6–5.0
	(mph)
gradient	1.1 (fpm)
scenery	C+

DESCRIPTION: This section has limited access. However, canoe camping is a possibility. Paddlers can overnight at Blue Licks Battlefield State Park, where the river forms the western boundary of the park. It is 12 miles from the KY 32 bridge down to Blue Licks Battlefield State Park and 24 more miles to Claysville.

ABOUT THE SHUTTLE: To reach the upper access from Exit 121 on I-64, take KY 36 West to Carlisle. From Carlisle, take KY 32 East to Cassidy Creek Road, just before bridge over Licking River. Turn right on Cassidy Creek Road and put in at the bridge over Cassidy Creek.

GAUGE: Call the U.S. Army Corps of Engineers at (606) 784-9709 to receive water release schedule from Cave Run Lake Dam. The minimum release needs to be 120 cfs.

Middle Fork of the Licking River
KY 32 to Claysville

CLAY WILDLIFE MANGEMENT AREA

Cassidy Ck. Rd.

N

Robertson Co.

Fleming Co.
Nicholas Co.

68

32

G

F

Blue Licks
Battlefield
State Park

1658

32

Goose Creek Pike

165

1244

68

1455

To
Carlisle

1455

1476

617

1244

1244

62

1244

1504

392

Nicholas Co.
Harrison Co.

19

H

Claysville

1284

62

Points	River Miles	Shuttle Miles
F—G	12.16	7.29
G—H	24.31	17.16

CLAYSVILLE TO FALMOUTH

class	I
gauge	Web
level	Min. 120 Max. flood (cfs)
velocity	2.6–5.0 (mph)
gradient	1.0 (fpm)
scenery	C+

DESCRIPTION: This section also has limited access. The North Fork Licking River comes in 10 miles below Claysville, substantially increasing the flow. It is 7 miles farther down to the McKenneysburg Road Bridge. It is 15 miles from the McKenneysburg Bridge to Falmouth.

GAUGE: The USGS gauge is Licking River at McKenneysburg, KY. The minimum reading should be 120 cfs.

Middle Fork of the Licking River
Claysville to Falmouth

159

22

Falmouth

J

Bishop
Ridge
Rd.

McKenneysburg Rd.

1053

539

539

I

27

*North
Fork*

Pendleton Co.

Bracken Co.

Robertson Co.

Harrison Co.

1284

19

Claysville

1284

1504

H

62

Points	River Miles	Shuttle Miles
H—I	17.16	11.73
I—J	15.02	9.3

G

62

HINKSTON CREEK

A major tributary of the South Fork of the Licking River, Hinkston Creek originates in western Bath County and flows northwest along the Bourbon–Nicholas County line before joining Stoner Creek near Ruddels Mills.

MAPS: Carlisle, Millersburg, Shawhan (USGS)

MILLERSBURG TO CONFLUENCE WITH STONER CREEK

class	I
gauge	Web
level	Min. 150 Max. flood (cfs)
velocity	2.6–5.0 (mph)
gradient	1.6 (fpm)
scenery	B

DESCRIPTION: Flowing over a mud and gravel bottom between 12–15-foot mud banks, Hinkston Creek winds through gently rolling farmland. Much of the streamside is tree-lined, and several varieties of tall grasses can also be found. Runnable from November to early June downstream of Millersburg, the creek is Class I with some sandbars and frequent midstream islands covered with scrub vegetation. Surrounding countryside is historically interesting with numerous stone fences, many old homes, and a covered bridge. Average stream width is from 30 to 40 feet, and access is fair to good. Logjams and deadfalls are the primary hazards to navigation (you must put in below a 5-foot dam if starting in Millersburg).

GAUGE: The USGS gauge is Hinkston Creek near Carlisle, KY. The minimum reading should be 150 cfs.

Points	River Miles	Shuttle Miles
A—B	5.01	5.72
B—C	4.29	5.86
C—D	5.01	3.72
D—E	0.72	1.0

STONER CREEK

Stoner Creek drains central Bourbon County and runs north through Paris to its confluence with Hinkston Creek. Runnable from November to mid-June north of Paris and December through April south of Paris, Stoner Creek flows through some of the world's most famous thoroughbred horse farms.

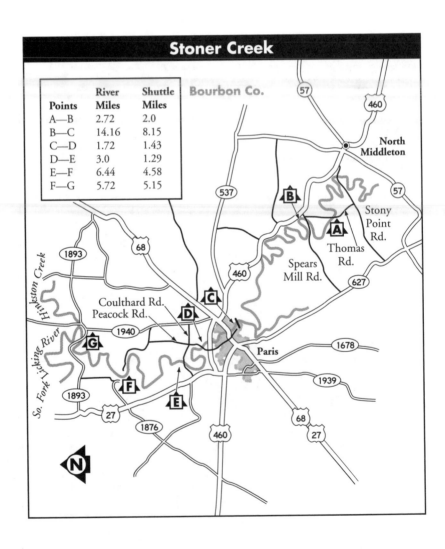

Points	River Miles	Shuttle Miles
A—B	2.72	2.0
B—C	14.16	8.15
C—D	1.72	1.43
D—E	3.0	1.29
E—F	6.44	4.58
F—G	5.72	5.15

THOMAS ROAD BRIDGE TO CR 1893 BRIDGE

class	I
gauge	Web and visual
level	Min. 160 Max. flood (cfs)
velocity	2.6–5.0 (mph)
gradient	2.4 (fpm)
scenery	B+

DESCRIPTION: The creek itself is primarily Class I. It has numerous grass islands and flows over a mud and rock bottom between steep, 15-foot banks. Access is good north of Paris, but in the upper sections of the stream, to the south of Paris, access is difficult, with most put-ins and take-outs located on private property. It is here, unfortunately, that the most interesting scenery occurs. Deadfalls are the primary hazards to navigation.

GAUGE: Using the USGS gauge for adjacent Hinkston Creek is helpful. The USGS gauge is Hinkston Creek near Carlisle. The minimum reading should be 160 cfs. However, this method lacks precision and should be used in conjunction with a visual check of the creek.

SOUTH FORK OF THE LICKING RIVER

The South Fork of the Licking River originates at the confluence of Hinkston and Stoner Creeks near Ruddels Mills, south of Cynthiana, and flows north over a limestone, mud, and sand bottom to join the North and Middle Forks of the Licking River near Falmouth.

MAPS: Shawan, Cynthiana, Breckenridge, Berry, Goforth, Falmouth (USGS)

South Fork of the Licking River
Ruddels Mill to Berry

Points	River Miles	Shuttle Miles
A—B	7.87	7.15
B—C	5.86	2.15
C—D	13.28	10.01
D—E	10.15	7.29
E—F	5.01	5.29

RUDDELS MILLS TO BERRY

class	I
gauge	Web
level	Min. 3 (ft)
	Max. flood
velocity	1–2.5 (mph)
gradient	3.4 (fpm)
scenery	B

DESCRIPTION: Running in steep mud banks lined with silver maple and sycamore, the South Fork is Class I throughout with grass islands and numerous sandbars. The grass islands often form narrow channels that paddlers must navigate. Its average width is between 40 feet at its origin and 80–90 feet at its confluence with the other forks. The South Fork flows through the town of Cynthiana. Access to the river is generally good. Hazards to navigation include deadfalls as well as dams at Cynthiana, Poindexter, Robinson, and Berry (some of which exceed 5 feet in height). These must be portaged. Trips of varying lengths can be made on this river.

GAUGE: The USGS gauge is South Fork Licking River at Cynthiana. The minimum runnable reading is 3 feet.

BERRY TO FALMOUTH

class	I
gauge	Web
level	Min. 3 (ft)
	Max. flood
velocity	1–2.5 (mph)
gradient	3.2 (fpm)
scenery	B

DESCRIPTION: This section has even more grass islands and channels. These channels vary with the water level, necessitating a different route at different levels. Access to the river is generally good. Hazards to navigation include deadfalls as well as the dam at Falmouth, which must be portaged on the right. The dam at Falmouth is a popular fishing hole. Below the dam are some of the most continuous shoals on this section. Thaxton's Licking River Canoe Rental (phone (859) 472-2000 or visit www.go paddling.com) can provide shuttle on the South Fork.

ABOUT THE SHUTTLE: To reach take-out from the intersection of US 27 and KY 22, take KY 22 East into downtown. Where KY 22 turns right, at the intersection with Main Street and just after Shelby Street, keep forward and follow gravel road down to The Point, where the South Fork and Licking River meet.

GAUGE: The USGS gauge is South Fork Licking River at Cynthiana. The minimum runnable reading is 3 feet.

South Fork of the Licking River
Berry to Falmouth

Points	River Miles	Shuttle Miles
F—G	5.72	4.29
G—H	12.16	4.58
H—I	8.72	10.01
I—J	5.72	2.86

LICKING RIVER

The Licking River below the confluence of its three forks is a big river and is runnable all year. Its scenery is pleasant, with the river winding in lengthy curves through broad valleys bordered by tall hills and ridges.

MAPS: Falmouth, Butler, DeMossville, Alexandria, Newport, Covington (USGS)

FALMOUTH TO LOCUST PIKE PARK

class	I
gauge	Web
level	Min. 120
	Max. flood (cfs)
velocity	2.6–5.0 (mph)
gradient	1.2 (fpm)
scenery	C+

DESCRIPTION: The banks of the Main Licking, as it is locally known, are generally steep on one side and sloping on the other. Flat terraces occur frequently about 5 feet up from the water line. Its average width is 190 to 220 feet Trees, mostly hardwoods, line the banks. For a large, navigable river, there is a conspicuous absence of powerboat traffic, due to shoals and the scarcity of access points. Below the US 27 bridge through Kenton County north to Newport, where the Licking River empties into the Ohio River, the railroad effectively monopolizes the west bank. Beyond the sprawling switchyards, steep ridges make it almost impossible to reach the water. Along the east bank in Campbell County, large farms and other types of private property buffer the stream. Comparatively long distances between access points, then, limit this section's attractiveness to paddlers. The level of difficulty is Class I throughout, and occasional floating debris represents the only hazard to navigation. Access, as mentioned, is scarce but is reasonably good where it exists. Thaxton's Canoe Rental operates on US 27 in Butler.

Licking River
Falmouth to Locust Pike Park

N

17
275
D
27
Locust Pike
Park
9
177
Alexandria
1930
10
16
C
1930
536
1303
1936
2042
Kenton Station Rd.
14
2046
Cambell Co.
Kenton Co.
17
177
Pendleton Co.
177   159
609
17
27
27
A
159
22   Falmouth
22
330
22
South Fork
Licking River

Points	River Miles	Shuttle Miles
A—B	20.02	12.87
B—C	17.88	16.47
C—D	7.2	10.01

ABOUT THE SHUTTLE: To reach the Locust Pike Park access, take US 27 and follow it north to KY 536. Turn left on KY 536 West to reach KY 177. Turn right on KY 177 North and follow it to KY 1930. Turn right on KY 1930 and follow it to Locust Pike. Turn left on Locust Pike and follow it to boat ramp on right.

GAUGE: The USGS gauge is Licking River at Catawba, KY. The minimum reading should be 120.

part**Three**

THE KENTUCKY RIVER AND ITS TRIBUTARIES

NORTH FORK OF THE KENTUCKY RIVER

The North Fork of the Kentucky River originates in the mountains of southeastern Kentucky near Whitesburg and flows northwest, draining the counties of Letcher, Perry, Breathitt, and Lee. There are 140 paddleable miles before the North Fork meets the South Fork and Middle Fork in Beattyville. This is a bona fide mountainous coal country, where the only flat land is directly along any watercourse slicing through the hills. The North Fork is no exception, and much of the streamside is settled or farmed. The North Fork is runnable in its upper reaches (Roxana to Viper) during the winter and early spring only. Downstream, from Viper to Jackson, the river can be paddled from late October to mid-June. Below Jackson, the North Fork of the Kentucky is usually runnable all year.

MAPS: Roxana, Blackey, Vicco, Hazard South, Hazard North, Krypton, Haddix, Quicksand, Jackson, Tallega, Campton, Zachariah, Beattyville (USGS)

ROXANA TO VIPER

class	I–II
gauge	Web
level	Min. 150
	Max. flood (cfs)
velocity	2.6–5.0 (mph)
gradient	7.0 (fpm)
scenery	B

DESCRIPTION: In the upper sections, the river is 35–40 feet wide and flows over a mud and gravel bed through steep, wooded valleys and coal country. As Line Fork enters the stream at the Perry–Letcher County line, water volume increases significantly, and the river widens to approximately 55–60 feet. Although the terrain is rugged, humans and their habitat are visible all along the upper North Fork. Trees overhang the stream in the extreme upper section (above Blackey) but give way to thick scrub vegetation further downstream. Paddling is interesting, with numerous small shoals and rapids (Class I+). Deadfalls pose the only major peril to navigation.

North Fork of the Kentucky River
Roxana to Viper

Points	River Miles	Shuttle Miles
A—B	6.44	6.44
B—C	5.72	5.72
C—D	2.36	1.79
D—E	5.36	5.01
E—F	4.86	5.86

VIPER TO CHAVIES

class	I
gauge	Web
level	Min. 175 Max. flood (cfs)
velocity	2.6–5.0 (mph)
gradient	2.8 (fpm)
scenery	B

GAUGE: The USGS gauge is North Fork Kentucky River at Whitesburg. The minimum reading should be 150 cfs.

DESCRIPTION: This section of the North Fork passes through the growing town of Hazard. The gradient is less than the upper section, but shoals keep you moving along. Though detracting from the wilderness atmosphere, the small towns, frame houses, wooden footbridges, and porch-front rockers present an enduring and picturesque perspective of eastern Kentucky mountain living. The river itself is winding and has steep banks that make access generally difficult, even at bridges. Difficulty notwithstanding, additional access points along the section make trips of varied distances possible. Much of the river can be scouted from KY 15 south of Hazard. As KY 15 intersects the river south of Hazard, the North Fork sinks into increasingly deep banks. Even with a highway on the west and a railroad on the east, access is difficult. Scenery, however, remains beautiful.

GAUGE: The USGS gauge is North Fork Kentucky River at Whitesburg. The minimum reading should be 175 cfs.

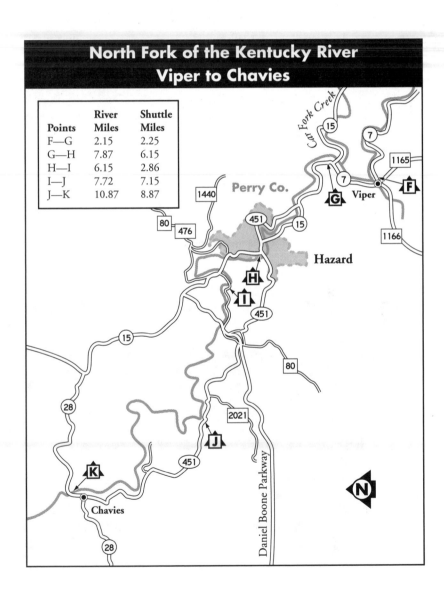

North Fork of the Kentucky River
Viper to Chavies

Points	River Miles	Shuttle Miles
F—G	2.15	2.25
G—H	7.87	6.15
H—I	6.15	2.86
I—J	7.72	7.15
J—K	10.87	8.87

CHAVIES TO JACKSON

class	I
gauge	Web
level	Min. 175 Max. flood (cfs)
velocity	2.6–5.0 (mph)
gradient	2.7 (fpm)
scenery	B–

DESCRIPTION: The water's quality diminishes below Hazard due to mining discharge, and there is less vegetation along the banks. Signs of human habitation are more frequent and the scenery far less picturesque than farther upstream. The river valley broadens here, and farm fields become more common. Rapids and shoals disappear as the stream settles into mud banks. Access is somewhat limited the first 17 miles below Chavies, however, after that access can be had on the KY 1110 bridge, along KY 15 and KY 1812. The latter two roads parallel the North Fork here.

GAUGE: The USGS gauge is North Fork Kentucky River at Whitesburg. The minimum reading should be 175 cfs.

North Fork of the Kentucky River
Chavies to Jackson

Points	River Miles	Shuttle Miles
K—L	17.16	17.88
L—M	5.72	6.44
M—N	5.72	5.58
N—O	5.86	5.01

JACKSON TO BEATTYVILLE

class	I
gauge	Web
level	Min. 260
	Max. flood
	(cfs)
velocity	2.6–5.0
	(mph)
gradient	2.65 (fpm)
scenery	C+

DESCRIPTION: As the North Fork flows north through Jackson toward Beattyville, the surrounding hills (known locally as mountains) become smaller and the river widens to an average of 80 feet and expands to 110 feet at its confluence with the Middle Fork of the Kentucky. Though runnable all year, this section lacks the intimacy and beauty typical of the upper sections. Alternative access points include the KY 541 bridge and the KY 2016 bridge. Between these two bridges is a 30-mile stretch with no public access.

ABOUT THE SHUTTLE: The take-out in Beattyville is located just west of the KY 52 bridge over the North Fork. Look left just on the west side of the bridge for River Road. Turn left here and look left for a small public park next to the Beattyville City Hall, an old house.

GAUGE: The USGS gauge is North Fork Kentucky River at Whitesburg. The minimum reading should be 260 cfs.

North Fork of the Kentucky River
Jackson to Beattyville

Points	River Miles	Shuttle Miles
O—P	12.16	7.15
P—Q	32.18	22.17
Q—R	7.15	6.01

MIDDLE FORK OF THE KENTUCKY RIVER

The Middle Fork of the Kentucky River originates in the southeastern Kentucky mountains of Leslie County and flows north through the tip of Perry County into Buckhorn Lake, and from there north through Breathitt County into Lee County, where it joins the North Fork of the Kentucky near Beattyville.

MAPS: Hoskinston, Cutshin, Hyden East, Hyden West, Buckhorn Canoe, Cowcreek, Tallega, Beattyville (USGS); Daniel Boone National Forest, Central Section

WAR BRANCH TO BUCKHORN LAKE

class	I–II
gauge	Web
level	Min. 175 Max. flood (cfs)
velocity	2.6–5.0 (mph)
gradient	13.7 (fpm)
scenery	C+

DESCRIPTION: The upper waters of the Middle Fork roll out of the hills in the western portion of Leslie County in the Daniel Boone National Forest. Although the upper reaches are crowded with small mountain communities, the river valley and surrounding hills are nevertheless extremely beautiful.

The river flows over a rock and gravel bed with almost continuous Class I+ and Class II rapids and shoals. Runnable in late winter and early spring, the upper section is paralleled by KY 1780, from which the run can be scouted. Hazards, including deadfalls, low bridges, and concrete fords, are easily spotted. The river is small, averaging 25–35 feet in width. Banks are 6–10 feet in height and easily traversed; access is good. The riverside of the banks is well vegetated, but most trees are situated somewhat back on the floodplain away from the river, providing the mixed blessing of being able to see both the human habitation and the truly spectacular surrounding hills ("mountains") as you paddle along.

Near the intersection of KY 1780 and US 421, the river collects several major tributaries and proceeds to follow US 421 north toward Hyden. This section is also characterized by extremely mild whitewater (Class I+), but it is of a more intermittent nature. Access once again is good, and the scenery is much improved as the river moves away from the line of houses and barns that dot the headwaters. Runnable from late November to early June, this section passes through beautiful wilderness hill terrain before emerging in Hoskinston. Beyond Hoskinston and Stinnett, the river again slips into the forest to rejoin civilization in Hyden. Occasional deadfalls and a 5-foot dam as the river approaches the Leslie County High School complex south of Hyden are the only dangers to navigation.

At Hyden, the river averages 50 feet in width and has descended into a luxurious green valley sprinkled with cabins on the hills overlooking the river. Its banks are mud and are extremely tall and steep. Above the steep banks a gorge rises with exposed rock visible. This can best be appreciated during the colder months when the foliage of trees along the banks does not

Middle Fork of the Kentucky River
War Branch to Buckhorn Lake

Points	River Miles	Shuttle Miles
A—B	2.72	2.72
B—C	1.43	1.43
C—D	3.0	3.0
D—E	1.29	1.29
E—F	2.5	2.5
F—G	11.44	8.58
G—H	7.15	7.87
H—I	3.72	4.29

obstruct the view. From Hyden to Buckhorn Lake, the river smooths considerably and has only a few riffles and small waves. Access is good where it is available. Hyden City Park is an excellent access point. This section is normally runnable from November to early June. Trace Branch Recreation Area on Buckhorn Lake, which has camping, is just down the lake from Confluence Recreation Area.

GAUGE: The USGS gauge is Middle Fork Kentucky River at Tallega. The minimum reading should be 175 cfs.

BUCKHORN DAM TO BEATTYVILLE

class	I
gauge	Web
level	Min. 210 Max. flood (cfs)
velocity	2.6–5.0 (mph)
gradient	1.7 (fpm)
scenery	C+

DESCRIPTION: From the tailwaters of the Buckhorn Dam to the mouth of Turkey Creek in Breathitt County, the river widens somewhat but otherwise remains essentially the same. Habitation along the Middle Fork increases sharply along this section as the river departs the national forest. This section is runnable almost all year, and access is good. The shuttle route follows the river almost the entire way and makes trips of varied lengths easy.

From the mouth of Turkey Creek (near Guerrant) to the Lee County line, the Middle Fork flows through hilly woods and farm country, but population is sparse, and fewer dwellings are visible from the river. Between Turkey Creek and its confluence with the North Fork of the Kentucky, the Middle Fork swells to 110–130 feet in width. Like the North Fork, the Middle Fork in Lee County lacks the dramatic scenery and continually changing vistas of the upper sections.

GAUGE: The USGS gauge is Middle Fork Kentucky River at Tallega. The minimum reading should be 210 cfs.

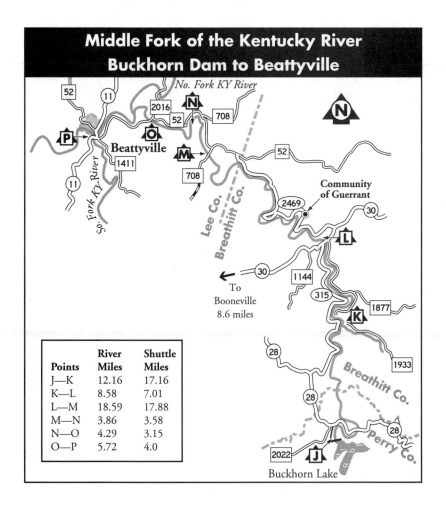

Middle Fork of the Kentucky River
Buckhorn Dam to Beattyville

Points	River Miles	Shuttle Miles
J—K	12.16	17.16
K—L	8.58	7.01
L—M	18.59	17.88
M—N	3.86	3.58
N—O	4.29	3.15
O—P	5.72	4.0

RED BIRD RIVER

The Red Bird River is the main tributary of the South Fork of the Kentucky River. Running over a bed of rock, gravel, and mud, the Red Bird winds through the Daniel Boone National Forest, draining the eastern half of Clay County.

MAPS: Creekville, Big Creek (USGS); Daniel Boone National Forest, Central Section

QUEENSDALE TO SOUTH FORK KENTUCKY RIVER

class	I+
gauge	Visual
level	Min. 180
	Max. flood (cfs)
velocity	2.6–5.0 (mph)
gradient	7.2 (fpm)
scenery	B

DESCRIPTION: Runnable in late fall and spring, the river can best be described as a busy Class I with almost continuous riffles, small waves, and shoals. At higher water, several of the shoals and small rapids may be classified as borderline Class II. The Red Bird valley is one of the most beautiful in the Daniel Boone National Forest, with steep hills looming above the river and lush vegetation everywhere. Some human habitation is in evidence along the Red Bird River, but it does not usually detract from the beauty of the stream. Banks are 5–8 feet high and of varying steepness. Access is good from the Red Bird Hospital to the KY 80 bridge, as roads parallel the Red Bird the whole way. This allows for scouting and trips of varied lengths. Average width is 30–40 feet throughout, and concrete fords and deadfalls represent the only navigational hazards.

GAUGE: Nearly the entire river can be scouted by parallel roads. The Red Bird should be runnable when the South Fork Kentucky is a little high.

Red Bird River

	River	Shuttle
Points	Miles	Miles
A—B	2.57	2.17
B—C	3.65	3.43
C—D	3.58	4.2
D—E	2.43	3.02
E—F	7.87	6.44
F—G	3.5	3.0

SOUTH FORK OF THE KENTUCKY RIVER

The South Fork of the Kentucky River originates at the confluence of the Red Bird River and Bullskin Creek (at Eriline) in Clay County and flows north over primarily mud banks through Owsley County to its confluence with the North and Middle Forks of the Kentucky River, near Beattyville in Lee County.

MAPS: Big Tree, Mistletoe, Oneida, Booneville, Beattyville (USGS); Daniel Boone National Forest, Central Section

ERILINE TO BEATTYVILLE

class	I (II)
gauge	Web
level	Min. 225
	Max. flood (cfs)
velocity	2.6–5.0 (mph)
gradient	3.3 (fpm)
scenery	B

DESCRIPTION: From the mouth of the Red Bird River to Oneida, the South Fork averages 35–50 feet in width and is primarily Class I with some occasional small shoals. The surrounding scenery is very pleasant as the river meanders through a broad valley bordered with high, wooded hills. Access is fair (at best) in this section because of a scarcity of crossings and high, steep banks. Vegetation is thick and trees line the streamside. Navigational hazards consist mainly of deadfalls.

North of Oneida (which is further downstream), the banks remain very high and steep. Trees are less frequent at streamside, and much of the surrounding floodplain has been terraced and farmed. The river is less scenic here than upstream, but the general absence of trees along the immediate banks allows a good view of the bordering hillsides.

Approximately 3 miles north of Oneida, near Teges, the river turns sharply to the east away from KY 11 (which follows the stream downstream of Oneida and offers numerous access points) into a dense, secluded woodland. From here to the Clay–Owsley County line lies the most scenic and interesting paddling of the entire South Fork. Runnable from November to mid-June, this section is alive with small shoals and several borderline Class II rapids. Sloping hillsides bring the forest right down to the river bank. Average width is 45–55 feet and access is good. Navigational dangers are limited to an occasional deadfall, concrete fords, and low-water bridges.

As the South Fork flows through Owsley County, leaving behind the national forest, it encounters broader valleys, scenic, pastoral farmland, and increased human habitation. Riffles and shoals are infrequent here and disappear altogether after the South Fork passes Booneville. Between Booneville and its confluence with the North and Middle Forks, the South Fork averages 70–90

South Fork of the Kentucky River

Beattyville

Middle & North Fork
Kentucky River

K

52

1411

Lee Co.
Owsley Co.

587

J

1411

Pine Grove Rd.

11

30

Booneville ← **I**

30

1938

11

28

H

2024

2025

Upper Wolf Creek Rd.

River Rd. **G**

846

1350

2024

Owsley Co.
Clay Co.

F

E

Rock School Rd.

Rocky Bridge Rd.

D

Newfound Rd.

Teges

11

C

Oneida

66

1482

Goose Creek

Bull's Kin Creek

N

11

B

66

Bear Creek Rd.

Eriline

A

149

Exit 34
Daniel Boone Parkway

Points	River Miles	Shuttle Miles
A—B	5.86	5.15
B—C	6.86	6.44
C—D	7.01	5.22
D—E	2.15	3.15
E—F	8.15	4.29
F—G	7.72	5.72
G—H	1.43	1.0
H—I	10.73	7.01
I—J	7.87	7.15
J—K	5.72	5.01

feet in width and is runnable all year. Access is fair to good. It is 13 miles from Eriline to Oneida, 36 miles from Oneida to Booneville, and 14 miles from Booneville to Beattyville.

ABOUT THE SHUTTLE: The access in Beattyville is just west of the KY 52 bridge over the North Fork Kentucky River. Turn onto River Dr. and follow it just a few feet to a park on the left, beside the Beattyville City Hall offices. You have to paddle upstream on the North Fork a very short distance below the KY 11 bridge on the South Fork to reach this access.

GAUGE: The USGS gauge is South Fork Kentucky River at Booneville. The minimum reading should be 225 cfs.

KENTUCKY RIVER BELOW THE FORKS

The Kentucky River from Beattyville to Frankfort would be a good canoeing stream were it not for the abundance of powerboats, both pleasure and commercial. The Kentucky River is scenic, running first through forested hills and well-kept farmland, later curving beneath 400-foot exposed rock palisades, and finally emerging into a broad, fertile plain bordered by tall, wooded ridges. Access is plentiful and usually good. Dangers to navigation include ten dams (exclusive of No. 4 below Frankfort), floating debris, and of course, the ever-present armada of powercraft. A Class I river, the Kentucky is runnable all year. Its banks are mud and usually steep. Numerous trip possibilities exist along this stretch. Highlights includes historic Camp Nelson downstream of Lock 8, High Bridge, and the mouth of the Dix River below Dix Dam (Herrington Lake) just upstream of Lock 7, and the City of Frankfort (the capital of Kentucky) above Lock 4.

Visitors are welcome at all of the locks, and the lock grounds are suitable for picnicking, putting in, or taking out. Two locks (10 and 8) have beaches adjoining them. You can usually leave shuttle vehicles parked at the locks while you're running the river, but be sure to check with the lockmaster to find out what time the grounds are closed. Be aware that locks 6, 8, 9, 10, 11, 12, 13, and 14 have been closed until further notice.

When approaching the locks from the river, all must obviously be portaged. This presents no problem except at Lock 5, where no good landing areas exist. If you expect to portage Lock 5, carry two 30-foot lengths of line to hoist your boat up the side of the lock (there will be a ladder for you). If you are in a large group or arrive at the lock at the same time as a powerboat, the lockmaster will normally allow you to lock through. Though not as fast as carrying around, locking through is fun and interesting, particularly if there are children in the group.

MAPS: New Liberty, Worthville, Vevay South, Carrollton, Frankfort East, Frankfort West, Polsgrove, Switzer, Gratz, Salvisa, Tyrone, Valley View, Little Hickman, Buckeye, Wilmore, Harrodsburg, Panola, Palmer, Union City, Winchester, Ford, Richmond North, Valley View (USGS)

BEATTYVILLE TO IRVINE

class	I
gauge	Web
level	Min. 600
	Max. flood (cfs)
velocity	2.6–5.0 (mph)
gradient	0.7 (fpm)
scenery	C+

DESCRIPTION: The forks of the Kentucky River gather at Beattyville to form the Kentucky, averaging 80–105 feet wide here. This upper stretch is in coal country. A railroad parallels the river its entire length. Lock 14 is encountered 3 miles below Beattyville. The KY 399 bridge is 4 miles farther. Lock 13 is 10 miles below KY 399. It is 21 miles between Lock 13 and Lock 12, and 4 more miles to Irvine.

GAUGE: The USGS Gauge is Kentucky River at Lock 14/Heidelberg. The minimum reading should be 600 cfs.

Kentucky River
Beattyville to Irvine

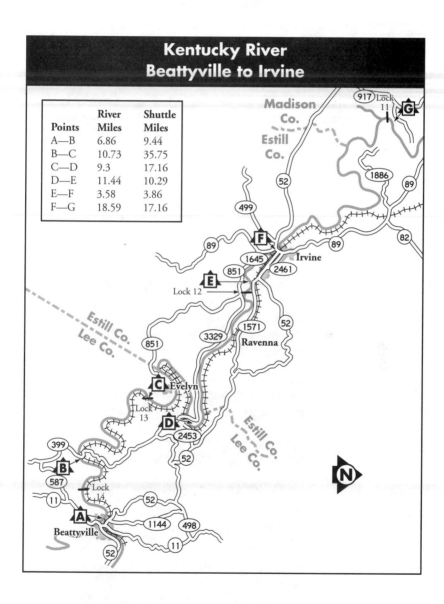

Points	River Miles	Shuttle Miles
A—B	6.86	9.44
B—C	10.73	35.75
C—D	9.3	17.16
D—E	11.44	10.29
E—F	3.58	3.86
F—G	18.59	17.16

IRVINE TO
VALLEY VIEW FERRY

class	I
gauge	Web
level	Min. 600 Max. flood (cfs)
velocity	2.6–5.0 (mph)
gradient	0.7 (fpm)
scenery	C+

DESCRIPTION: Points of interest include Fort Boonesborough State Park (with beach and campground) just below Lock 10, and a 30-foot waterfall one-half mile up Boone Creek (entering the Kentucky River on the right just upstream of the I-75 bridge). The river averages 95–125 feet wide on this stretch. It is 18.5 miles from Irvine to Lock 11. The Red River comes in 10 miles below Lock 11. It is 16.5 miles to Fort Boonesborough State Park and Lock 10 from the Red River, and 20.5 miles farther to Valley View Ferry from the park.

GAUGE: The USGS Gauge is Kentucky River at Lock 14/Heidelberg. The minimum reading should be 600 cfs.

Kentucky River
Irvine to Valley View Ferry

Points	River Miles	Shuttle Miles
G—H	10.01	18.59
H—I	6.66	13.59
I—J	7.15	24.31
J—K	2.86	2.72
K—L	7.87	10.01
L—M	12.87	14.3
M—N	0.72	0.72

VALLEY VIEW FERRY TO LOCK 6

class	I
gauge	Web
level	Min. 800 Max. flood (cfs)
velocity	2.6–5.0 (mph)
gradient	1.0 (fpm)
scenery	B

DESCRIPTION: The most scenic run between Beattyville and Frankfort is between Lock 8 and Lock 7, where magnificent exposed rock palisades grace the river on both sides. This can be made into a canoe-camping run with an overnight stop at Camp Nelson. Numerous small tributary streams worthy of exploration enter the river between Lock 9 and Lock 8.

Lock 9 is less than a mile below the put-in. Valley View Ferry is the oldest continually operating business in the state, ongoing since 1785, and is the only ferry remaining on the Kentucky River. Continuing downriver, Lock 8 is 21 miles distant from Lock 9. Camp Nelson is 5 miles below Lock 8. The Dix River confluence is 20 miles below Camp Nelson and 1.5 miles above Lock 7. There are no access points between Lock 7 and Oregon boat ramp, almost 21 miles

ABOUT THE SHUTTLE: To reach Lock 6 access from Harrods-burg, head north on US 127, beginning to look for Oregon Road after passing KY 1985. Turn right on Oregon Road and follow it to turn left on Oregon Landing Road to reach Oregon boat ramp, on the right. To reach Valley View Ferry access from Harrodsburg, take US 68 East to KY 29. Head east on KY 29 to US 27 Business. Turn left, north on US 27 Business, and follow it to KY 169. Turn right on KY 169, Richmond Avenue, and follow it to Valley View Ferry. A private boat launch is just upstream of the ferry.

GAUGE: The USGS Gauge is Kentucky River at Lock 10/ Winchester. The minimum reading should be 800 cfs.

Points	River Miles	Shuttle Miles
M—N	0.72	0.72
N—O	9.3	20.02
O—P	4.22	9.3
P—Q	7.29	7.15
Q—R	5.01	11.73
R—S	20.02	21.59
S—T	1.43	1.43
T—U	20.74	25.74
U—V	1.72	1.72

LOCK 6 TO KENTUCKY RIVER VIEW PARK

class	I
gauge	Web
level	Min. 800 Max. flood (cfs)
velocity	2.6–5.0 (mph)
gradient	1.0 (fpm)
scenery	B

DESCRIPTION: The river averages 110–135 feet wide. This section has one lock to portage, Lock 5, above Clifton. It is 17 miles from Lock 6 to Lock 5, and 19 more miles to Frankfort.

ABOUT THE SHUTTLE: To reach the lowermost access in Frankfort, take US 421 North, Wilkinson Boulevard, from US 127 to Kentucky River View Park, which has a small boat launch.

GAUGE: The USGS Gauge is Kentucky River at Lock 10/Winchester. The minimum reading should be 800 cfs.

Kentucky River
Lock 6 to Kentucky River View Park

Benson Creek

421
421
127

BB

460

1005

60

Frankfort

N

Franklin Co.
Woodford Co.

1659

460

420

64

1681

1659

Buckley
Wildlife
Sanctuary

AA

127

2331

1964

60

62

Anderson Co.

151

Ninevail Clifton Rd.

Clifton

1659

326

Y

Z

1964

Versailles

127

Lock
5

62

60

Lawrenceburg

44

1510

X

Wildcat Rd.

Shyrock Fy. Rd.

1964

62

127

Bluegrass Pkwy.

33

W

1965

Exit 59

513

Anderson Co.
Mercer Co.

1964

Lock
6

Points	River Miles	Shuttle Miles
V—W	8.58	12.87
W—X	5.01	15.73
X—Y	3.58	6.51
Y—Z	3.29	11.44
Z—AA	7.15	17.16
AA—BB	7.01	8.44

V

Oregon Rd.

1987

Oregon Rd.

127

KENTUCKY RIVER VIEW PARK TO LOCK 2

class	I
gauge	NA
level	Min. 457 Max. flood (cfs)
velocity	2.6–5.0 (mph)
gradient	0.5 (fpm)
scenery	B–

DESCRIPTION: Below Frankfort, the Kentucky River continues through farm valleys bordered by steep ridges. The level of difficulty remains Class I. Access is generally good. Lock 4 is just below the put-in, and Lock 3 is near Monterey. Both of these locks must be portaged.

ABOUT THE SHUTTLE: From Frankfort, take US 127 North to KY 355. Turn left and take KY 355 North to Gratz and KY 22. Turn left and take KY 22 West to KY 389 South. Turn left on KY 389 South and follow it to Lock 2. A boat ramp is just above the lock. To reach the uppermost access in Frankfort, take US 421 North, Wilkinson Boulevard, from US 127 to Kentucky River View Park, which has a small boat launch.

GAUGE: The locks make the river runnable year-round. The normal pool stage for below Lock 4 is 457.1 feet.

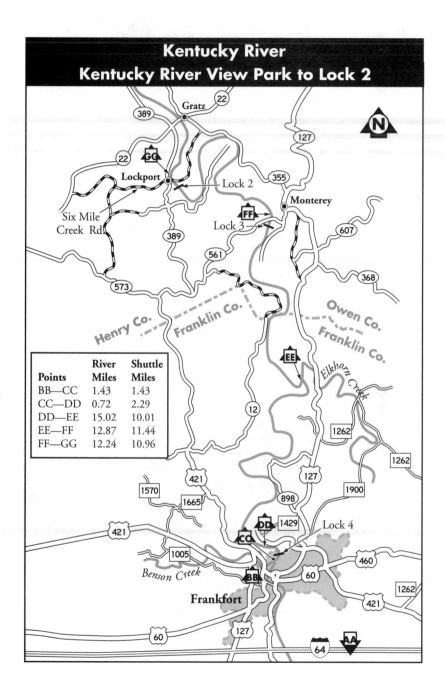

Kentucky River
Kentucky River View Park to Lock 2

Points	River Miles	Shuttle Miles
BB—CC	1.43	1.43
CC—DD	0.72	2.29
DD—EE	15.02	10.01
EE—FF	12.87	11.44
FF—GG	12.24	10.96

**LOCKPORT TO
CARROLLTON BOAT DOCK**

class	I
gauge	Web
level	Min. N/A
	Max. flood
velocity	2.6–5.0
	(mph)
gradient	0.5 (fpm)
scenery	B

DESCRIPTION: The Kentucky River is at its widest and largest here, ranging from 140 to 200 feet Lock 1 is just above Carrollton. The take-out is on the Ohio River, upstream of the mouth of the Kentucky River, in historic Carrollton.

GAUGE: The USGS gauge is Kentucky River at Lock 2/Lockport. However, the locks keep the river runnable all year.

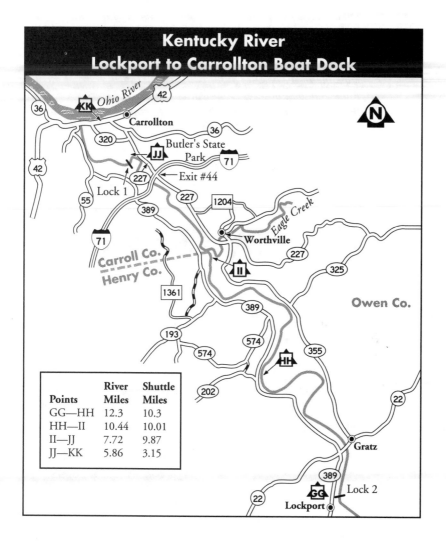

Kentucky River
Lockport to Carrollton Boat Dock

Points	River Miles	Shuttle Miles
GG—HH	12.3	10.3
HH—II	10.44	10.01
II—JJ	7.72	9.87
JJ—KK	5.86	3.15

RED RIVER

Originating in Wolfe County, the Red River flows northwest through Powell County and along the Estill–Clark County line before emptying into the Kentucky River south of Winchester. During the early 1970s, national attention was focused on the river and on the beautiful Red River Gorge through which it flows, when Kentuckians and conservationists from throughout the country successfully fought the U.S. Army Corps of Engineers over the building of a dam. Hanging in the balance as the battle raged was the heart of the Red River and some of the most spectacular canoeing waters anywhere in the eastern United States. For paddling purposes, the Red River is popularly divided into three sections: the Upper, the Middle, and the Lower Red River.

MAPS: Lee City, Cannel City, Hazel Green, Pomeroyton, Slade, Stanton, Caly City, Palmer (USGS); Daniel Boone National Forest map, North Section

UPPER RED RIVER

class	II (III)
gauge	Web
level	Min. 200 Max. 350/500 open/decked (cfs)
velocity	2.6–5.0+ (mph)
gradient	13.29 (fpm)
scenery	A+

DESCRIPTION: The Upper Red River is a Class II–III whitewater stream of unparalleled beauty winding among boulders and beneath cavernous overhangs. Only 20 feet wide at the put-in near the Big Branch access, the Upper Red remains intimate throughout, with hardwoods shading the water and mountain laurel growing thick above the rock ledges. The first 3 miles are scenic Class I water with a good current and a few small riffles and ledges. Below the mouth of Stillwater Creek, the gradient increases with a technical Class II rapid.

From here downstream the Red winds below imposing bluffs, assuming a pattern of alternating pools and small rapids (Class I+), with the only interruption coming in the form of a riverwide ledge ranging from 1.5 to 1.5 feet in height and often referred to as the Falls. This ledge is sometimes difficult to get over at low to moderate water levels and is best run far left or far right. Continuing downstream, the river remains well behaved until it reaches the mouth of Peck Branch. For the next half-mile, the Upper Red twists through a series of three borderline Class III rapids, popularly known as the Narrows of the Red. The first rapid is a long series of ledges with a healthy sampling of rocks to dodge, ending with a 2.5-foot plunge into a beautiful pool. Enter at the top left center, skirt the obstructing rocks as the water level allows, and pull into the eddy behind the last midstream rock before the vertical drop. Run the vertical drop by hugging the large boulder on the far left. The second rapid, 30 yards downstream, is known as Dog Drowning Hole and should probably be scouted (on the right). It consists of a turning chute accompanied by a great deal of turbulence. At low water it is very technical, and at higher water very squirrelly with irregular waves and currents. The total drop along the length of this rapid is approximately 5 feet. At the third rapid of the Narrows, the river appears to come to a dead-end. The current is deflected along the upstream face of a large boulder to the left bank, where it cuts right, down a fast sluice with an inclined 3-foot drop, finally washing up on an undercut rock 30 feet downstream. Run the sluice right center and grab an eddy on the right before the undercut rock grabs you. From here downstream to the take-out at the KY 715 bridge, the run is an easy Class II with delightful scenery and lots of hikers and back-packers to wave at.

The Upper Red is runnable from late December to late May in years of average rainfall. At very low water the run can turn into a hike; however, the now established USGS gauge at Hazel Green should eliminate most treks. At very high water the Red is extremely dangerous, practically running in the trees. Rapids on the Red are not especially difficult, but on the other hand they allow little margin for error. Dangers other than those already described include frequent deadfalls, several undercut rocks, and the potential of the river to rise rapidly following a rain. The best time to run the Upper Red is in the morning because of the after-noon sun that shines directly into your eyes after about 2 p.m. An emergency walk-out exit can be found on river-right shortly after the Falls of the Red. Look for the steel cables from an old swing-ing bridge over the river. Here, a rough path leads north out of the gorge onto farmland.

ABOUT THE SHUTTLE: From Exit 40 on Mountain Parkway, take KY 15 North toward Slade to KY 715. Turn right and head north on KY 715 down to the Copperas Creek River Access on the Red. A national forest parking fee is required here. To reach the put-in from Exit 43 on Mountain Parkway, take KY 15 South to KY 191 East. Keep on KY 191 through Campton to reach KY 746. Turn right and follow KY 746 North past the bridge over the Red to KY 3357, Sandfield Road. Turn right on Sandfield Road and look for a signed right turn onto a gravel road and the Big Branch River Access. Do not use the KY 746 bridge for an access, as it is posted.

GAUGE: The USGS Gauge is Red River near Hazel Green. The minimum reading should be 200 cfs.

MIDDLE RED RIVER

DESCRIPTION: The middle section of the Red River begins at KY 715 bridge and twists through the center of the Red River Gorge; past Sky Bridge Arch, Tower Rock, and Chimney Top Rock; and works its way between boulders in the stream, eventually ending in the shadow of Raven Rock at the KY 77 bridge. Its

class	I+
gauge	Web
level	Min. 180 Max. flood (cfs)
velocity	2.6–5.0 (mph)
gradient	2.5 (fpm)
scenery	A

Red River
Middle Red River

Points	River Miles	Shuttle Miles
B—C	8.0	7.6

level of difficulty is Class I throughout, but numerous sharp turns, sandbars, riffles, and small ledges make the paddling interesting. The scenery is spectacular without exception, with enormous hardwoods shading the stream and wildflowers in abundance. The middle section of the Red is runnable from late fall to early summer most years. Access is excellent. Navigational hazards consist of deadfalls, occasional logjams, and periodic overcrowding.

GAUGE: The USGS Gauge is Red River at Clay City. The minimum reading should be 180 cfs.

LOWER RED RIVER

class	I
gauge	Web
level	Min. 180
	Max. flood (cfs)
velocity	2.6–5.0 (mph)
gradient	2.5 (fpm)
scenery	B

DESCRIPTION: The Lower Red River, downstream of KY 77, remains very scenic for the first several miles, winding along below Courthouse Rock and finally running out of the Red River Gorge. From here downstream, the river is pleasant and meanders through hilly farm country and woodlands, but it does not compare to the upper and middle sections. Additionally, the lower section is almost always clogged with deadfalls that force portaging or swinging continually back and forth across the river to navigate around them. Flowing over a bed of gravel and mud between steep banks, the Lower Red is bordered by private property and is not suitable for camping. However, access points are numerous from bridges aplenty crossing the Red, availing day trips of varied lengths. Aside from deadfalls and logjams, there are no other navigational hazards. The Lower Red River averages 35–55 feet in width and is runnable from late fall to early summer.

GAUGE: The USGS Gauge is Red River at Clay City, KY. The minimum reading should be 180 cfs.

Red River
Lower Red River

Points	River Miles	Shuttle Miles
C—D	9.1	8.2
D—E	3.0	3.9
E—F	4.7	3.5
F—G	8.6	4.6
G—H	5.7	2.0
H—I	14.2	10.4
I—J	2.5	5.4

FOUR MILE CREEK

This is one of the first creeks to look for when the other whitewater creeks in the Clark/Madison County area are also running high. However, rains can be highly localized. The entire run is scoutable from the road and at moderate levels offers whitewater consisting of a very playful set of diagonal holes for the novice-intermediate boater. At higher levels this fast runoff stream contains numerous Class III hydraulics that will provide strong playboaters added fun and novices, increased trepidation.

MAPS: Winchester (USGS)

Four Mile Creek

Points	River Miles	Shuttle Miles
A—B	5.0	4.2

BYBEE ROAD TO KENTUCKY RIVER

class	II–III (IV)
gauge	Visual
level	Min. 3 in. Max. 2 ft.
velocity	2.6–5.0+ (mph)
gradient	40 (fpm)
scenery	A

DESCRIPTION: Much of the bank along the roadside of the creek has been concreted in, keeping the road from eroding the way during high water but also making the creek seem like a drainage ditch. However, the creek itself is made up of numerous limestone ledges. The last half-mile of the run is on the Kentucky River.

SHUTTLE: To reach Four Mile Creek from Winchester, take KY 1923 West to Bybee Road. Continue forward on Bybee Road until it comes to a T intersection at Four Mile Road and Four Mile Creek. Put in here, or turn left to signed Dead End Road that leads to a ford on Four Mile Creek and the property of boater-friendly landowner Alice Rankin. To reach the take-out, backtrack from signed Dead End Road and follow Four Mile Road until it curves around to Kentucky River. Good parking and decent landing on the Kentucky River are available past a small iron truss bridge that spans a feeder branch of Kentucky River.

GAUGE: What you see is what you get. If Howard's Creek is running, Four Mile Creek is most likely running.

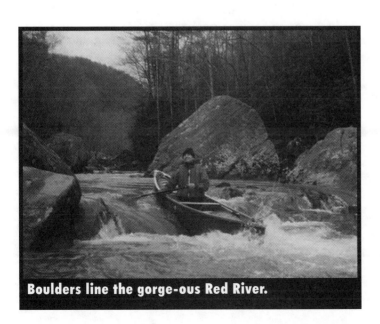

Boulders line the gorge-ous Red River.

LOWER HOWARD'S CREEK

Lower Howard's Creek is one of central Kentucky's most beautiful, interesting, and historic whitewater streams. Running through a narrow, remote, and lush gorge, the stream features remains of eighteenth-century architecture, including stone mill races, pioneer houses, and mills. Furthermore, this stream boasts almost continuous Class II–III rapids and numerous play places from the put-in to the take-out.

MAPS: Ford, Winchester (USGS)

OLD STONE CHURCH ROAD TO KENTUCKY RIVER

class	II–III (IV)
gauge	Visual
level	Min. 3 in. Max. 2 ft.
velocity	2.6–5.0+ (mph)
gradient	40 (fpm)
scenery	A

DESCRIPTION: Even with its copious whitewater attributes, Lower Howard's Creek is not a run for paddlers with weak rolls, who lack of precision boat control, or who are inattentive to downstream hazards. Even at moderate flows of 1 foot over the road, Howard's could be upgraded to a solid Class IV stream with many blind turns; small, infrequent eddies; as well as numerous and ever-changing deadfalls, strainers, fences, and cables that require multiple portages.

ABOUT THE SHUTTLE: To reach the take out from Exit 96 on I-64, north of Winchester, take US 627 South to KY 418. Turn left and take KY 418 West under KY 627 Bridge to Halls Restaurant. Park here. To reach the put-in, backtrack to KY 627 and head north back to Old Stone Church Road. Turn left on Old Stone Church Road and follow it to a low-water bridge over Howard's Creek. Do not block roads or cross bridge at parking area.

GAUGE: The gauge is where Old Stone Church Road crosses Lower Howard's Creek. Minimum level is 3 inches of water over the road, maximum is 2 feet of water over road.

Lower Howard's Creek

Points	River Miles	Shuttle Miles
A—B	5.1	5.5

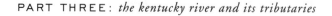
BOONE CREEK

Boone Creek is a small, intense stream flowing over a rock bed along the eastern border of Fayette County. Runnable only 10 or 12 days a year, it just may be the most singularly beautiful run in the entire state. The upper section (above the Iroquois Hunt Club) snakes over ledges between 20-foot-high rock walls. Passing the hunt club, Boone Creek's gradient increases as it descends into a narrow, vertical-walled rock gorge that funnels the stream at furious speed toward its mouth at the Kentucky River. Frequently, the constricting gorge walls recede, permitting trees to grow along the water's edge. At higher water levels these trees create the only eddies on the run. Feeder streams join Boone Creek at several points below the hunt club. Two of these enter the creek after dropping over large waterfalls that are easily visible from Boone Creek. During the spring, wildflowers, particularly bluebells, further enhance the beauty of the stream.

MAPS: Clintonville, Ford (USGS)

KY 418 TO KENTUCKY RIVER

class	II–IV
gauge	Visual
level	Min. 170
	Max. 400/900 open/decked (cfs)
velocity	2.6–5.0+ (mph)
gradient	31 (fpm)
scenery	A+

DESCRIPTION: Although Boone Creek may be beautiful, it is also dangerous. At higher water it is a continuous Class III run (which some have classified as Class IV due to the scarcity of eddies). Its gradient averages 31 fpm but ranges as high as 44 fpm in certain sections. The gradient is evenly distributed, and no single drops exceeding 3 feet are encountered. Strainers in the form of deadfalls and logjams present the greatest danger. Creek-wide farm fences may also occasionally appear in times of extended low water and then disappear completely or only partially be washed away in wet years. Fences are hazardous on any creek but particularly so on the Boone in light of the scarcity of eddies and the fast, pushy current at higher levels that allows very little time for the paddler to react. Action is continuous and consists primarily of standing waves, holes, and small drops, plus quick, twisting, and sometimes blind turns.

Boone Creek at high water is recommended only for experienced groups of two or more intermediate and advanced boaters with dependable rolls because rescue of swimming paddlers and their boats can be difficult among the vertical, tree eddy strainers. At moderate levels, Boone Creek is a good Class II to low Class III run. Parking at the 418 bridge put-in is limited to a small gravel road on river-left downstream. Permission is generally given to park on the side of that road if you do not block it. Access at Grimes Mill Road Bridge near the Hunt Club is not a good option; area is signed as no parking zone, and Hunt Club and homeowners are hostile to anyone parking there. Parking is abundant at the take-out on KY 2328. Dangers other than those mentioned include several undercut ledges. The last portion of the paddle is on the flat water of the Kentucky River, which may back up a considerable distance into Boone Creek during times of high water.

GAUGE: Boone Creek is runnable only after heavy rains, more often in winter and spring.

Boone Creek

Points	River Miles	Shuttle Miles
A—B*	2.2	3.4
B*—C	4.1	4.0

*No parking

HICKMAN CREEK

East and West Fork Hickman flow forth from Lexington's two reservoirs and collect water as they run out of Lexington to Jessamine County. The creek offers some good central Kentucky scenery with woodland and farmland views, similar to those found on Elkhorn Creek (while being a smaller stream). However, Hickman is not as clean as the Elkhorn, in fact in can be downright poor, and the nice view is occasionally disrupted by trash along the creek banks.

MAPS: Little Hickman (USGS)

KY 1541 TO ELM FORK ROAD

class	I-II
gauge	Web
level	Min. 600 Opt. 800–1,100 (cfs)
velocity	2.6–5.0 (mph)
gradient	10 (fpm)
scenery	B

DESCRIPTION: This section is less exciting than most central Kentucky whitewater streams. It can be better described as a float. However, paddlers need to note a good wave just upstream of the Elm Fork Road Bridge. Check this surfing waves around 7–9 hours after the gauge reads 700–1,100 cfs. The best surfing water level is hard to catch: It becomes difficult to reach the wave when the water is really high, but when the water is low, it becomes less inviting.

You can reach this wave as a park-and-surf option, but you do have to drive through water spilling onto the road at higher flow levels. Take a left on John Watts Ln., just before the take-out bridge (John Watts Ln. is a gravel road that looks like it is the driveway for a house surrounded by yard decorations. This is a county road.) After turning left on John Watts Ln., follow the road through the creekbed to an old junked car. Proceed upstream past this landmark approximately 200 yards and park on the rock shelf just downstream of an island and out of the road. Though the majority of this drive is over a stable limestone footing, be warned that it can be hazardous at high water. Frequent flooding results in constant change to this access. You better have a rugged vehicle with four-wheel drive and even then be very prudent about whether to drive into the water. Scouting before high water is a smart move.

GAUGE: The virtual gauge used, on the American Whitewater Web site (www.americanwhitewater.org), is a combination of East and West Hickman Creeks and offers a quick resource to check the future creek level. However, to attain the most reliable prediction, consult and add the individual USGS gauges for East Hickman at Delong and West Hickman at Ashgrove Pike, using the fixed-width table output format for gauge reading and time.

Both gauges are found above the commonly paddled sections and therefore are indicators of future flows. It usually takes 7–9 hours for the "virtual flow" to reach the take-out bridge on Elm Fork, although this will be affected by several factors beyond the scope of this description. The bare minimum reading is around 500 cfs for a float and 700 cfs for a park and surf. The maximum is around 1,500 cfs. Above 1,200 cfs, many of the best features begin to wash out and the creek takes on a flooded appearance.

Hickman Creek
KY 1541 to Elm Fork Road

	River	Shuttle
Points	Miles	Miles
A—B	4.2	5.7

ELM FORK ROAD TO KY 1268 BRIDGE

class	I–II (III)
gauge	Web
level	Min. 600 Opt. 800– 1,100 (cfs)
velocity	2.6–5.0 (mph)
gradient	21 (fpm)
scenery	B

DESCRIPTION: If you are in it purely for the whitewater, consider putting in at the ford on Brumfield Lane. Several rapids are just below this access, which is also a park-and-surf area. Your trip can be extended by putting in farther upstream at either Elm Fork Road, at Black Bridge on KY 39, or even at KY 1541. These longer trips will appeal to tandem canoeists, especially at lower water levels.

ABOUT THE SHUTTLE: To reach the take-out from Nicholasville, take US 27 south to KY 1268 (it will be the second 1268 as you head south from Nicholasville). Turn left and take KY 1268 to bridge over Hickman Creek. Parking is on the left, just before reaching the bridge. To reach the put-in, backtrack to Brumfield Ln., which may or may not be signed. It will be a very acute right-hand turn onto a paved road that looks like a driveway. Follow Brumfield Lane, passing Watts Mill Road that veers left. (Watts Mills Road can be used to access upstream put-ins, as it cuts across KY 39 near additional stream crossings.) Keep on Brumfield Ln. and follow it to wide, flat, and low-water bridge over Hickman Creek. If the water is near the upper flow limits or rapidly rising, you must park on the hill before reaching the bottomland that surrounds the creek and road ford, which will be impassable when paddling is a possibility. Four-wheel drive, decent ground clearance, and pre-high-water scouting are recommended.

GAUGE: The virtual gauge used, on the American Whitewater Association Web site (www.americanwhitewater.org), is a combination of East and West Hickman Creeks. Both gauges are found above the commonly paddled sections and therefore are indicators of future flows. It usually takes 8–10 hours for the "virtual flow" to reach the take-out bridge on KY 1268.

Hickman Creek
Elm Fork Road to KY 1268 Bridge

Nicholasville

Points	River Miles	Shuttle Miles
B—C	6.1	11.1

N

39

1541

39

West Ln.

3374

39

Elm Fork Rd.

27

39

Feck Ln.
Park
-n-
Surf

Watts Mill Rd.

1268

B

Watts Ln.

Black Bridge

Elm Fork Rd.

1268

ford

39

Brumfield Ln.

39

Pollard Pike

1268

Hickman Creek

C

39

Kentucky River

1268

Kentucky River

27

JESSAMINE CREEK

This stream offers a scenic paddle in close proximity to Nicholasville and south Lexington. It offers continuous twists and turns that are shrouded in overhanging trees and in the beginnings of a fairly deep gorge. There are also several interesting sites not found on other central Kentucky streams, including a postcard scenic stone bridge at the take-out and a primate rescue center in the last mile, where monkeys can be seen playing in tree-level cages.

MAPS: Wilmore (USGS)

FRANKFORT FORD ROAD TO KY 1268

class	II (III)
gauge	Visual
level	N/A
velocity	2.6–5.0 (mph)
gradient	33 (fpm)
scenery	A–

DESCRIPTION: At low water, Jessamine can be scrapy, as many of the rapids are rock shoals rather than the typical central KY limestone shelves. At high water it offers decent excitement (II–II+ and maybe III when huge) and a few nice surfing waves that develop at differing water levels. There is a right turn rapid approximately a half-mile into the trip, characterized by a rock outcropping that is fairly tight and could have a tendency to trap strainers. A couple other areas downstream are also narrow and could offer strainer traps and safety hazards. Additionally, there is a low-water road that crosses approximately halfway down from the put-in, and in the past there has been a chain stretched across the creek to keep drivers from venturing upstream at low water.

One rapid of note is very close to the take-out and is signaled by a right-hand rock wall and what appears to be a broken shelf or possibly old dam or ford. With big water, this sloping area can create a couple of diagonal waves that make a paddler forget he or she is only in central Kentucky and offer quite a thrill. Also, there is a low head dam (maybe 4–6 feet) just below the stone bridge at the take-out that is a safety hazard and bears mentioning. Although it has been run at medium flow, it could be very dangerous and offer a good chance of drowning, as low heads do. It is of note that the gorge downstream of this bridge is quite deep, with portions owned and reserved as conservation land. It is very scenic and offers significant eye and paddling appeal. However, access is limited, and it is therefore infrequently paddled.

ABOUT THE SHUTTLE: To reach the take-out from Nicholasville, take US 27 South to KY 1268. Turn right on KY 1268 North and follow it to stop sign. Turn left at stop sign, staying with KY 1268, to reach a one-lane bridge over Jessamine Creek. Parking is very limited here. There is room for one car near the bridge and more room if you turn left onto Figg Lane, or continue on KY 1268, beyond the bridge. To reach the put-in, back-track on KY 1268 to the stop sign. Continue forward past the stop sign, now on Frankfort Ford Road. Keep forward on Frankfort Ford Road to bridge over Jessamine Creek.

GAUGE: What you see is what you get. This creek runs only after heavy rains, particularly from late fall though spring leaf out. Jessamine Creek drains Nicholasville and surrounding developments, and takes a few hours to get from rainfall to put-in. That being said, several "viaducts" can be checked in down-town Nicholasville for a predictor of future flow.

DIX RIVER

The Dix River originates in Rockcastle County and flows northwest through Lincoln County before being impounded to form Herrington Lake along the Garrard–Boyle County line. From the Dix River Dam, the river flows a short 2 miles before emptying into the Kentucky River.

MAPS: Lancaster, Stanford, Bryantsvillle, Wilmore (USGS)

LOGANTOWN TO HERRINGTON LAKE

class	I++
gauge	Web
level	Min. 200 Max. flood (cfs)
velocity	2.6–5.0 (mph)
gradient	2.4 (fpm)
scenery	C+

DESCRIPTION: Flowing primarily through farmland and wooded hills, the Dix is a pleasant, intimate river shaded by hardwoods and occasionally graced with some small bluffs and exposed rock ledges. Running over a mud bottom in the upper stretches between often-steep mud banks, the streambed changes to a rock bottom with boulders along the bank as the Dix approaches the mouth of the Hanging Fork. Its level of difficulty is Class I, although several tight spots require good boat control. Riffles, small ledges, and shoals are not uncommon. Dangers to navigation consist mainly of deadfalls and occasional logjams. The Dix is runnable from late fall to late spring downstream of the US 27 bridge at Logantown. Other access points are KY 1150 and KY 52. Canoe camping is possible if adjoining sections of the river and lake are combined. Campgrounds are all privately owned and charge for camping space.

GAUGE: The USGS gauge is Dix River near Danville, KY. Minimum reading should be 200 cfs.

Dix River

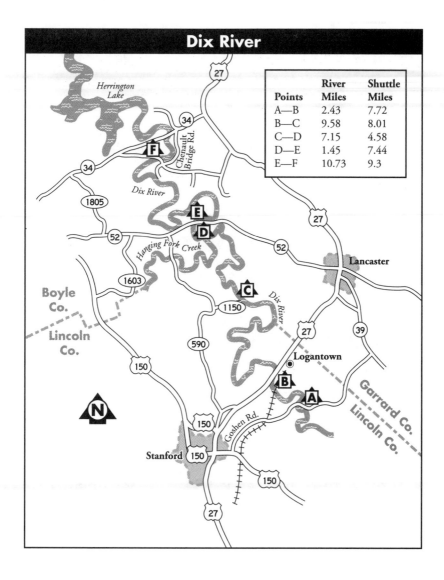

Points	River Miles	Shuttle Miles
A—B	2.43	7.72
B—C	9.58	8.01
C—D	7.15	4.58
D—E	1.45	7.44
E—F	10.73	9.3

HANGING FORK OF THE DIX RIVER

The Hanging Fork, a tributary of the Dix River flowing northeast along the Boyle–Lincoln County line, is runnable from late fall to early May below the KY 590 bridge. An interesting little stream (15–30 feet wide), the Hanging Fork twists through a small, shady gorge interrupted occasionally as grassy, grazing plains insinuate themselves between the steep ridges.

MAPS: Stanford (USGS)

KY 590 TO DIX RIVER AT KY 52

class	I (II)
gauge	Visual
level	Min. 120 Max. 400 (cfs)
velocity	2.6–5.0 (mph)
gradient	14 (fpm)
scenery	B

DESCRIPTION: The paddling is rated a busy Class I and borderline Class II with almost continuous small shoals and rapids. There are numerous deadfalls and immense logjams to avoid. Grass and brush is common around shoals. There is also a small dam near the confluence with the Dix that may be portaged or (at favorable water levels) run on the left where the dam is partially collapsed. Scout first! Emerging on the Dix River, the take-out is three-quarters of a mile downstream below the confluence with the Dix at KY 52 bridge.

GAUGE: If the Dix is running high and the water looks floatable at the KY 590 bridge on the Hanging Fork, the trip should be a go.

Boone Creek Gorge

Hanging Fork of the Dix River

Points	River Miles	Shuttle Miles
AA—E	5.72	1.72

GILBERT CREEK

Gilbert Creek is an often-overlooked paddle stream, probably due to its small watershed. Draining the southeastern corner of Anderson County, south of Lawrenceburg, Gilbert Creek flows into the Kentucky River. Load your boat after a heavy rainfall of two inches or more during winter or early spring. Be forewarned: With a gradient of 75 feet per mile, this is for serious boaters only.

MAPS: McBrayer (USGS)

GILBERT CREEK ROAD TO KENTUCKY RIVER

class	II–III+
gauge	Visual
level	N/A
velocity	2.6–5.0 (mph)
gradient	75 (fpm)
scenery	A

DESCRIPTION: This is not a creek for beginners. It starts fast and furious and never lets up. Limestone ledges are featured top to bottom. Because of its size and gradient, there are very few eddies. Take advantage of the shuttle to scout wherever you can. Much of the run can be scouted from the road. There are many trees to avoid and it is likely you will encounter deadfalls. Boat scouting is possible, but everyone in the group will have to fend for themselves, because what eddies that do exist will fill up quickly with one or two boats.

Be ready for play spots at any time—there are numerous surf waves and ledge holes the length of the run. If in doubt at any of the larger ledges, go left, where the current flushes out. The largest of the ledges is a 4-foot sloping ledge with a tongue on the left that is followed by a quick right turn. It can be seen from the road and is located just below a private bridge halfway along the run.

At about 2 miles there will be a small creek entering from the left. Gilbert Creek will narrow and begin to accelerate down a 50-yard stretch with a constant gradient. Every ounce of the creek's energy will become focused as it enters a large pool. The result is a startlingly large haystack wave that you must crash through. Be alert for the take-out on the left—there is a very bad hydraulic below the low-water crossing.

ABOUT THE SHUTTLE: From Exit 59 on the Blue Grass Parkway, take US 127 South just a short distance to KY 513. Turn left on KY 513 and follow it 2.7 miles to a private low-water bridge (1156 address). Park and put in just below the bridge. To reach the take-out, continue downstream on KY 513 to low-water bridge on KY 513 crossing Gilbert Creek. This bridge will be impassable when the creek is up.

GAUGE: The low-water bridge—visible from the Blue Grass Parkway. and the first one you will see on your right heading along the creek—has pipes running under it. It the pipes are more than half-full, then you should be in business.

Gilbert Creek

Points	River Miles	Shuttle Miles
A—B	2.75	2.7

BENSON CREEK

Benson Creek flows northeast out of Anderson County, through Franklin County to the Kentucky River at Frankfort. Runnable above the confluence of the forks after heavy rains and below the confluence from late fall through the spring, Benson Creek offers a variety of surprises. The waterway is often floated by locals when the water is up, generally November to mid-May following heavy rains.

MAPS: Frankfort West (USGS)

KY 1005 TO BENSON VALLEY BOAT RAMP

class	II–III
gauge	Visual
level	Min. 3 ft. Above 5.5 ft., experts only
velocity	2.6–5.0 (mph)
gradient	15.7 (fpm)
scenery	B+

DESCRIPTION: Concerning whitewater playboating, some say, "go big or go home." Benson Creek can get big, during its 10–20 times per year of being runnable, and then only for 4–10 hours at a time. When runnable, the North Fork, below Sheeppen Road, powers through fields and pastureland until suddenly it veers to the right and drops over a 13-foot vertical falls. However, two of the biggest rapids on the creek are here. One rapid, Big Bitch, is a deep hole where paddlers can do almost any freestyle move capable in a hole, including aerial loops. Another wave above the falls, Big Slut, is the only aerial wave in Kentucky. This is more of a low to moderate water level feature that is prime around 3–4 feet. Big Bitch is prime above 4.5 feet.

The South Fork, averaging only 20 feet in width downstream of the Pea Ridge Road put-in, drops swiftly over Class I and II ledges. Too many hard-to-see cattle fences and a lack of eddies make this run too dangerous at any water level no matter your level of expertise. The Falls of Benson should be run just left of center at moderate water levels.

Fortunately, Benson Creek below the confluence of the forks (just downstream of the large falls) is somewhat more predictable. Flowing between tall, beautiful, wooded bluffs (many with exposed rock), Benson Creek becomes a scenic and delightful Class II run with exceptional playboating river opportunities. Rapids consist primarily of riverwide ledges ranging from 1 to 3 feet in height that can be run just about anywhere. Holes occurring below the drops are generally friendly at most water levels. Several rapids disappear around curves and should be scouted for possible obstructions (deadfalls). Hazards include deadfalls, logjams, and a 5-foot low head dam at the distillery that should be portaged on the right. Some paddlers punch over the dam at one

Benson Creek

Frankfort

Kentucky River

Kentucky Ave.

Cline St.

West 2nd St.

421

60

1429

Lewis Ferry Rd.

1211

Taylor Ave.

1005

421

B Benson Creek
Boat Ramp

Benson Valley Rd.

127

Devils Hollow Rd.

McCann Rd.

1005

Bald Knob Rd.

421

1670

Benson Creek

Benson Valley Rd.

Devils Hollow Rd.

N

A

falls

1005

Points	River Miles	Shuttle Miles
A—B	4.5	4.1

of two holes because there is no hydraulic. The final half-mile or so of the run is on slack water before reaching the Benson Creek boat ramp.

ABOUT THE SHUTTLE: From downtown Frankfort, take US 127 South to KY 1211 South, then turn right on Benson Valley Road to reach the boat ramp on your right. To reach the put-in, return to US 127 and head south to turn right on Devils Hollow Connector and pick up KY 1005 West to reach bridge over Benson Creek just below the falls. However, there are no parking signs all around the bridge area, and tickets have been given for violation. Best option is to go upstream to access at KY 1665, where you can park across the railroad track on the side of gravel road to the right.

GAUGE: At KY 1005 bridge, Devils Hollow Road, near the falls. Minimum runnable level is 3.0, above 5.5 is for expert boaters only.

South Fork of Elkhorn Creek

Points	River Miles	Shuttle Miles
A—B	15.31	7.87

SOUTH FORK OF ELKHORN CREEK

Similar to the North Fork of Elkhorn Creek, the South Fork of Elkhorn Creek is also very seasonal, being runnable mostly during the winter and spring. Tree-lined and flowing through gently rolling terrain amidst fertile fields and picturesque Bluegrass horse farms, the South Fork can be paddled below (downstream of) Fishers Mill in Woodford County.

MAPS: Versailles, Midway, Frankfort East, Switzer (USGS)

FISHERS MILL TO FORKS OF ELKHORN

class	I+
gauge	Visual and phone
level	Min. 125 Max. flood (cfs)
velocity	2.6–5.0 (mph)
gradient	1.4 (fpm)
scenery	B–

DESCRIPTION: An exceptionally winding stream with continually changing vistas, the South Fork of Elkhorn Creek sports a variety of small riffles and ledges to enliven the paddling. Access is limited and the level of difficulty is Class I. Hazards to navigation include deadfalls and a large dam (portage right) near the confluence with the North Fork.

ABOUT THE SHUTTLE: To reach the Forks of Elkhorn from Frankfort, take US 60 East to US 460. Keep east on US 460 to KY 460 to reach KY 1689. Turn left on KY 1689 North, then immediately turn left on Schoolhouse Road to reach outfitter and put-in.

GAUGE: What you see is what you get. However, consider contacting Canoe Kentucky at the Forks of the Elkhorn for runnable level. Their number is (502) 227-4492.

NORTH FORK OF ELKHORN CREEK

The North Fork of Elkhorn Creek flows through Scott County and is runnable from late fall to late spring from Georgetown downstream. Several dams in the Georgetown vicinity create pools that permit the paddling of certain two- to four-mile stretches year-round.

MAPS: Georgetown, Midway, Stamping Ground, Switzer (USGS)

GEORGETOWN TO FORKS OF ELKHORN

class	1+
gauge	Web
level	Min. 180 Max. flood (cfs)
velocity	2.6–5.0 (mph)
gradient	4.0 (fpm)
scenery	B

DESCRIPTION: By and large, the North Fork winds through rolling farmland. Trees line the mud and rock banks that vary markedly in height and steepness. The most popular run on the North Fork begins at the covered bridge near Switzer and terminates at the confluence of the North and South Forks. In this stretch, the stream grows progressively rockier, and many small ledges and rapids appear (all Class I). Access is good all along the North Fork. Dangers to navigation include dams (as mentioned) that must be portaged and deadfalls. The dam just above KY 1688 has washed out and is now runnable. The level of difficulty is Class I throughout, the average width is 35–40 feet and access is excellent.

ABOUT THE SHUTTLE: To reach the Forks of Elkhorn from Frankfort, take US 60 East to US 460. Keep east on US 460 to KY 460 to reach KY 1689. Turn left on KY 1689 North, then immediately turn left on Schoolhouse Road to reach outfitter and put-in. To reach uppermost put-in at Georgetown, continue on US 460 East to Georgetown and bridge over North Fork. Look left, just after bridge for Oser Landing Park.

GAUGE: The USGS gauge is Elkhorn Creek near Frankfort, KY. The minimum reading should be 180 cfs.

North Fork of Elkhorn Creek

Points	River Miles	Shuttle Miles
A—B	2.0	2.1
B—C	5.15	4.29
C—D	6.86	4.43
D—E	6.58	7.15
E—F	7.58	3.72
F—G	7.78	4.29

ELKHORN CREEK

Elkhorn Creek, with its North and South Forks, flows northwest, draining portions of Jessamine, Fayette, Scott, Woodford, and Franklin Counties before emptying into the Kentucky River north of Frankfort. Because of its mild whitewater, beautiful scenery, plentiful access, and proximity to four major urban areas, the Elkhorn is Kentucky's most popular canoeing stream.

MAPS: Switzer, Polsgrove (USGS)

FORKS OF ELKHORN TO KENTUCKY RIVER

class	I+; whitewater section, II–III
gauge	Web
level	Min. 200 Max. 850/flood open/decked (cfs)
velocity	2.6–5.0 (mph)
gradient	9.5 (fpm)
scenery	B

DESCRIPTION: Northeast of Frankfort at Forks of Elkhorn, the two forks of Elkhorn Creek come together. Here begins the most popular and scenic of the Elkhorn's many offerings; 6 miles of lively Class II and III whitewater, altered by the massive flood of March 1997. Runnable from late fall to early summer, this 6-mile stretch is a perfect training ground for novice whitewater paddlers. Running through a deep gorge with exposed rock walls (sometimes reaching 200 feet in height), the rapids, riffles, and ledges are almost continuous. In all, there are four legitimate Class III rapids on this run with perhaps six additional high Class I or borderline Class IIs. Several islands punctuate the stream. All except the first at the very beginning of the run are normally run along the right side. At low water the run is technical and helpful in developing water-reading skills. At high water (3 feet) large standing waves predominate. Access is good. Dangers to navigation include a dam (mandatory portage, on left) adjacent to the Jim Beam Distillery, low-hanging branches, and occasional logjams.

Downstream of the whitewater section, the Elkhorn is runnable year-round. It continues swift and beautiful, flowing over a rock bed as it moves toward its rendezvous with the Kentucky. This final section clears the rocky gorge and drops into an intimate valley. Ledges, riffles, and small rapids persist, as do some more, fairly large islands. The stream's width fluctuates widely in this section from a constricting 35 feet to a broad and shallow 90 feet. Access is good, and deadfalls and logjams are the only navigational dangers. The level of difficulty is Class I.

ABOUT THE SHUTTLE: Put-in for the whitewater run below the forks of the Elkhorn is private. It is at the KY 460 bridge river-right, just upstream of the bridge. To park and put-in at the bridge, pay at the Elkhorn Creek Campground office just upstream on the South Fork of the Elkhorn.

Take-out for the whitewater run is on Peaks Mill Road (KY 1900). There is a take-out owned by AW (donated by local paddlers) on the left just before Knight's Bridge over the Elkhorn.

GAUGE: The USGS gauge is Elkhorn Creek near Frankfort, KY. The minimum reading should be 200 cfs.

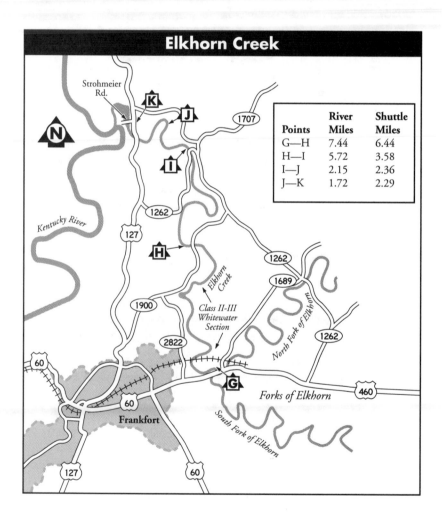

Elkhorn Creek

Strohmeier Rd.

Points	River Miles	Shuttle Miles
G—H	7.44	6.44
H—I	5.72	3.58
I—J	2.15	2.36
J—K	1.72	2.29

Kentucky River

Elkhorn Creek

Class II-III Whitewater Section

North Fork of Elkhorn

Forks of Elkhorn

Frankfort

South Fork of Elkhorn

EAGLE CREEK

Eagle Creek originates in Scott County and flows northwest over a mud and rock bottom through Owen, Grant, Carroll, and Gallatin Counties before emptying into the Kentucky River near Worthville.

MAPS: Lawrenceville, Elliston, Glencoe, Sanders, Vevay South, Worthville (USGS)

KY 36 BRIDGE TO KENTUCKY RIVER

class	I+
gauge	Web
level	Min. 190 Max. flood (cfs)
velocity	2.6–5.0 (mph)
gradient	4.7 (fpm)
scenery	C

DESCRIPTION: Runnable from November through May downstream of the KY 36 bridge in Grant County, Eagle Creek flows through the farmland and woods of the Northern Kentucky Knobs. Throughout the upper stretches of the stream (upstream of Sparta), the Eagle flows through a broad and frequently saturated floodplain. Banks are inclined gently in this section allowing seasonal rains to flatten all streamside vegetation. Brush islands formed on river curves following the recession of high water are common and provide navigational challenge to the paddler.

Below (downstream of) Sparta, the 45-foot stream runs more deeply as steeper banks channel the flow, and some very small ledges and rapids are encountered. The banks are treelined all along the Eagle but very thinly so. The level of difficulty is Class I throughout with deadfalls being the foremost danger to paddlers. Access is excellent between the KY 36 bridge and Worthville.

GAUGE: The USGS gauge is Eagle Creek at Glencoe, KY. The minimum reading should be 190.

Eagle Creek

Points	River Miles	Shuttle Miles
A—B	6.44	7.29
B—C	1.0	0.57
C—D	3.47	2.43
D—E	7.14	8.01
E—F	6.86	7.15
F—G	3.86	3.58
G—H	10.87	10.01
H—I	1.43	3.29

part**Four**

CREEK DRAINAGES OF MADISON COUNTY

CALLOWAY CREEK

This creek is also referred to—erroneously—as Galloway Creek. Calloway Creek plunges into the Kentucky River near the I-75 bridge south of Lexington. Runnable below the confluence of Smith Fork, this creek was first descended by local Kentucky paddlers in 2002. Calloway Creek ranks as one of the most scenic and intense whitewater streams in the Bluegrass State.

MAPS: Ford, Richmond North (USGS)

SMITH FORK TO KENTUCKY RIVER

class	II–IV
gauge	Visual
level	Min. N/A
	Max. N/A
	velocity 3–5
(mph)	
gradient	80 (fpm)
scenery	A+

DESCRIPTION: Calloway Creek boasts numerous nonstop, steep, vertical, and chaotic Class IV slide-style rapids through a spectacular high-walled canyon. There are two swinging-type cattle fences that an alert paddler may be able to pass under, depending on flow levels. Also, be apprised of creek-wide tree strainers.

First-time paddlers of Galloway should possess good boat scouting skills or should follow a Calloway veteran because there are numerous horizon lines with poor bank scouting possibilities. Calloway Creek enters the Kentucky River directly across from Boone Creek. The last part of the paddle is on the Kentucky River.

GAUGE: There is no gauge for Calloway Creek, but this stream can be visually checked following a significant rain event that brings the rest of Madison County's whitewater streams into runnable levels.

MUDDY CREEK

Muddy Creek is considered by many to be the best whitewater play stream in central Kentucky. With a drainage area of 63 square miles, Muddy Creek usually has a lag time of 3 hours or more following a heavy rain and will typically remain running for 12 to 24 hours. If you are able to run Tates Creek or any of the branches of Otter Creek, then the Muddy is probably flowing as well.

MAPS: Union City, Moberly (USGS)

OAKLEY WELLS ROAD BRIDGE TO NEAR DOYLESVILLE

class	II (III)
gauge	Visual
level	Min. N/A
	Max. N/A
velocity	3–5.5 (mph)
gradient	20 (fpm)
scenery	B

DESCRIPTION: Although it lacks any single, large drop or difficult rapid, Muddy Creek provides more surfing/freestyle fun per mile than any other whitewater run in the Bluegrass. Several small waterfalls add to the scenic quality of this run, which consists of mostly Class II–III easy and wide open rapids, with the very first rapid being the most difficult of the run. The Muddy contains hundreds of small ledges, forming essentially nonstop surfing waves and holes along its entire length. Many drops offer no-wait surfing for even for the largest of paddling groups. A riverwide hydraulic in the upper third of the run has several surfing boaters at once, confirming its name of Five Boat Hole. There is also a nice, single hydraulic park and surf in sight of the bridge where Cain Springs Road crosses the creek. At levels above "Suck" (see Gauge info) the Muddy tends to wash out, losing its great surfing. Hazards include the standard: strainers, brush piles, and floating debris.

ABOUT THE SHUTTLE: To reach the put-in take KY 52 East from Richmond to KY 977. Turn left and take KY 977 to Oakley Wells Road. The normal put-in can be reached by following Oakley Wells Road around the right-angle turn at the put-in. Do not go straight downstream on the dirt/gravel lane; that is a private drive. Park adjacent to the private drive on Oakley Wells Road. To reach the take-out, head west on Oakley Wells Road to Charlie Norris Road and turn right into beautiful downtown Union City. Turn right again at the small market onto KY 1986, the Union City Expressway, and follow it into Doylesville. Here, KY 1986 makes two 90-degree bends—first right, then left—keep forward on a dead-end road, as Weddles Mill Road turns right. Reach a bridge over Muddy Creek. Park in the gravel area

on left of bridge before crossing the bridge. If you cross Muddy
Creek or reach the Doylesville Church, you have gone too far.
Please do not block traffic.

Muddy Creek

Points	River Miles	Shuttle Miles
A—B	5.0	8.6

Intermediate access can be found at the park and surf where Cain Springs Road crosses the creek. From the intersection of College Hill Road (KY 977) and Oakley Wells Road, continue north on KY 977 to Cain Springs Road, at the Cain Springs Primitive Baptist Church. Turn left down the hill to the creek crossing.

GAUGE: Check the Cain Springs Road Bridge. Look for the word suck painted by a vandal on the upstream bridge support. If the water is within 12 inches of suck then the creek is a runnable level.

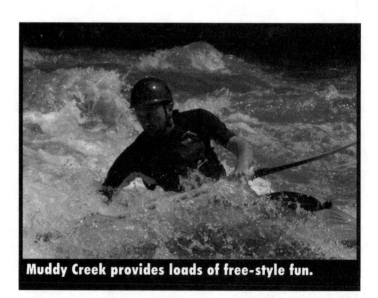

Muddy Creek provides loads of free-style fun.

WEST FORK/MAIN STEM OF OTTER CREEK

The West Fork/Main Stem of Otter Creek provides quality whitewater with few difficulties for novice or skilled paddlers. It is a short distance from the put-in on Bill Eads Road to the confluence with the Main (Middle) Stem of the Otter where the water volume doubles.

MAPS: Richmond North (USGS)

BILL EADS ROAD TO SAM JONES ROAD

class	II (III)
gauge	Visual
level	Min. N/A
	Max. N/A
velocity	3–5.5 (mph)
gradient	22.6 (fpm)
scenery	B

DESCRIPTION: The West Fork and Main Stem of the Otter is a very playful watershed littered with great surfing spots throughout its entire length. Easy, wide-open Class II rapids and the occasional Class III hydraulic prove Otter Creek to be another example of Madison County's wonderful whitewater bounty. Higher levels on the Otter will produce plenty of beautiful, large, smooth and glassy surfing waves as well as several large, sticky hydraulics easily boat scouted and avoided or surfed by skilled intermediate whitewater paddlers.

There are several alternate take-outs along its run to the Kentucky River, including the KY 3377 (Lost Fork Road) bridge, the confluence of the East Fork at KY 388, Sam Jones Road, and the KY 388 bridge close to Fort Boonesboro State Park.

ABOUT THE SHUTTLE: The take-out is reached by continuing downstream on KY 388 from Red House to where a small paved road directly beside a house, Sam Jones Road, leaves KY 388 on the left down a steep hill at a sharp angle downstream. The take-out is just beyond the uncontrolled railroad crossing, on river right, underneath the bridge crossing Otter Creek. Do not go across the bridge; this is a private drive.

The standard put-in for Otter can be reached by taking Exit 90 on I-75 and taking the US 421/25 Bypass to KY 1986. Turn left on KY 1986 and follow it a short distance to KY 388, Red House Road. Follow KY 388 to Red House. Turn left off KY 388 at the Red House Church, onto Bill Eads Road. Drive several hundred yards upstream on river left and park at a turn-out on your left where Bill Eads turns right, away from the creek. Please park so as not to block the gravel access road to a field.

GAUGE: Check the bridge piling on KY 3377, Lost Fork Road. Zero inches is the minimum runnable level.

West Prong/Main Stem of Otter Creek

EAST PRONG OF OTTER CREEK

Beginning as a narrow, intimate class II stream, the East Prong of the Otter soon joins up with a small tributary just upstream of the bridge at East Prong Road. From this point, the creek then rushes swiftly through several significant Class III drops (IVs at high water) to the confluence at the Main Stem of the Otter. With a drainage area of only 15 miles, the East Prong of the Otter comes up and down very fast. Due to its relatively short length, it is usually run in tandem with the Main Stem of Otter Creek past the KY 388 (Red House Road) bridge, offering an additional two to three miles of Class II–III whitewater. Note that there is another Otter Creek in Meade County that flows directly into the Ohio River.

MAPS: Richmond North (USGS)

EAST PRONG ROAD TO KY 388

class	II–III (IV)
gauge	Visual
level	Min. N/A
	Max. N/A
velocity	3–5.5 (mph)
gradient	35.7
scenery	B

DESCRIPTION: The East Prong has continuous whitewater with numerous play possibilities, interesting broken limestone shelf drops and some of the steepest gradients around central Kentucky. Hazards along the East Prong include deadfalls, sticky

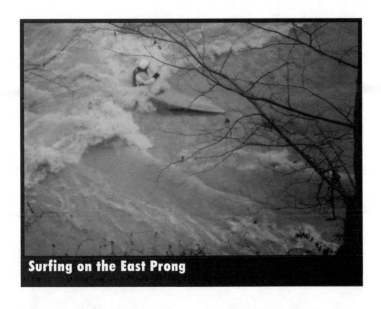

Surfing on the East Prong

East Prong of Otter Creek

hydraulics at higher water levels, low clearance under a driveway bridge, and a second low-head dam-style driveway. Both driveways should be scouted from East Prong Road when water levels are very high.

ABOUT THE SHUTTLE: There are two alternative put-ins on the East Prong. To gain the most creek mileage, take Peacock Road east from its intersection with KY 388 just north of the Redhouse Grocery. Follow Peacock Road until it crosses the East Prong of the Otter. Put in at the bridge, taking care not to block the road. For the most popular shuttle used to run only the steepest section of the East Prong, take KY 388 to East Prong Road about 3 miles north of Redhouse Grocery. East Prong Road follows the East Prong of the Otter until it dead-ends at the bridge across the East Prong. Please park on the river left side of the bridge, because the river right side is private land. There are two main take-outs (although other possibilities exist). Use the KY 388 bridge across the East Prong of the Otter. This makes for the shortest run of the East Prong of the Otter and is typically used at low to moderate flow levels when runs on other Madison County streams are planned. Or use KY 388 bridge across the Main Otter near Boonesboro State Park. This is usually the preferred take-out when water levels are very high and there is no sense in stopping the fun. Use of this take-out allows for several miles of the Main Otter to be run in conjunction with the East Prong.

GAUGE: The only way to gauge this creek is to look at it.

SILVER CREEK

Silver Creek boasts the largest watershed (112 square miles) of all of the Madison County whitewater streams and therefore will be most likely to hold its flow after a good rain. When doing a whitewater paddling Tour de Madison following a deluge rainfall, it is best to hold off on Silver Creek until the last and check out the other nearby streams first. East Prong Otter, Main Otter, Muddy, and Tates will all rise and drop at much faster rates than Silver Creek. After a moderate rain, when most of the others may not be running, look to Silver Creek first. Silver Creek consists of two main sections with the upper section containing a short park and surf section, allowing paddlers several options for paddling ranging from an all day tour to a short, no-shuttle-needed, play-filled half-mile.

MAPS: Kirksville, Richmond South (USGS)

CURTIS PIKE BRIDGE TO KY 876 BRIDGE

class	I–III (IV)
gauge	Visual
level	Min. 0
	Opt. 1–2 ft.
	Max. 4 ft.
velocity	2.5–5 (mph)
gradient	25 (fpm)
scenery	A

DESCRIPTION: Silver Creek runs through scenic lush forest, beautiful rolling hills, and well-groomed farmland with the half-mile above the KY 876 bridge containing the popular park and surf section for play-centric boaters that contains several surfing spots and rapids, including Silver Creek Falls, which can be easily scouted from KY 876 just upstream of the bridge.

Silver Creek Falls

At optimum flows of 0 inches to 2 feet, paddlers will discover Silver Creek to be littered with numerous playful hydraulics among mostly Class II+ limestone ledge drops plus a very scenic and runnable 4-foot riverwide ledge, locally known as Silver Creek Falls. At higher flows of 2–3 feet, Silver Creek approaches Class III through its short park and surf section. When gauge readings are 4 feet and higher, the swift, pushy water produces huge waves, increased possibility of large floating tree strainers and logjams, plus a significant but punchable recirculating hydraulic forming in the ledge of the third rapid in the park and surf section. Running just left of center and punching the hydraulic with strong momentum will help avoid getting caught in the very sticky right side.

ABOUT THE SHUTTLE: The standard put-in is on a tributary of Silver Creek, Taylor Fork, which drains a fishing impoundment called Wilgreen Lake. The put-in is reached from Exit 87 on I-75 by heading west on KY 876, Barnes Mill Road. From Barnes Mill, turn left onto Curtis Pike and follow it to a small paved road that leads to the dam at Wilgreen Lake. Turn left and park alongside the road. Taylor Fork lies in the woods across Curtis Pike. If Taylor Fork is too low, continue on Curtis Pike to where a concrete bridge crosses Silver Creek and put in there. To reach the take out from Exit 87 on I-75, take KY 876, Barnes Mill Road, west from the interstate to Bogie Mill Road, which continues straight on river right where Barnes Mill crosses Silver Creek from right to left on a concrete bridge, just beyond the Silver Creek Falls.

GAUGE: Check the visual gauge on KY 876 bridge over Silver Creek. Zero inches is minimum runnable level, with 1–2 foot optimum level.

KY 876 BRIDGE TO END OF BOGIE MILL ROAD

class	II
gauge	Visual
level	Min. 0
	Opt. 1–2 ft.
	Max. 4 ft.
velocity	2–4 (mph)
gradient	13 (fpm)
scenery	B

DESCRIPTION: The creek continues to be scenic, with herons and other bird species present along the way. The drops are not as frequent or steep as the upper section, but any time spent paddling Silver Creek will not be deducted from the rest of your life.

ABOUT THE SHUTTLE: From Exit 87 on I-75, take KY 876, Barnes Mill Road, west from the interstate to Bogie Mill Road, which continues straight on river right, where Barnes Mill crosses Silver Creek from right to left on a concrete bridge, just beyond the Silver Creek Falls. Follow Bogie Mill along the creek for about 2 miles, and continue on past Eddington Ln. to where a low-water ford crosses over to farmland. Park take-out vehicles near the ford, making sure not to block access to it, though at high water levels the ford would obviously be impossible. The put-in is on Barnes Mill just before it crosses Silver Creek on the aforementioned concrete bridge.

GAUGE: Check the visual gauge on KY 876 bridge over Silver Creek. Zero inches is minimum runnable level, with 1–2 foot optimum level.

TATES CREEK

With one of the smallest drainage areas in Madison County, Tates Creek will crest and fall quickly and should be among one of the first a paddler should look for immediately following torrential rains. Though Tates typically is only runnable only for a few hours, this creek is well worth the avid play boater's time. If you like fast water and big playable wave trains, then this is your stream.

MAPS: Richmond North, Valley View (USGS)

MILLION TO KY 169 BRIDGE

class	II–III
gauge	Visual
level	Min. N/A
	Max. N/A
	(cfs)
velocity	2.6–5 (mph)
gradient	30 (fpm)
scenery	B

DESCRIPTION: Tates Creek is one of the most accessible of Madison County's creeks, as it flows completely alongside KY 169, Tates Creek Road, just a few miles from I-75 and Richmond, KY. This stream is essentially a continuous series of non-stop Class II–III surfing waves and holes with very few flat sections or defined drops. At high water levels, the flow is a fast, pushy freight train, producing huge waves that form up into groups in the steeper, narrower sections. Tates does not tend to wash out at flood levels, and higher water only means larger more defined waves, holes, and fun for competent whitewater paddlers. Hazards along Tates Creek include strainers, especially along the section just upstream of the KY 1985 bridge that cannot be scouted from the road.

GAUGE: Check the water level at the Million Church—if it is over the road, you are on your own.

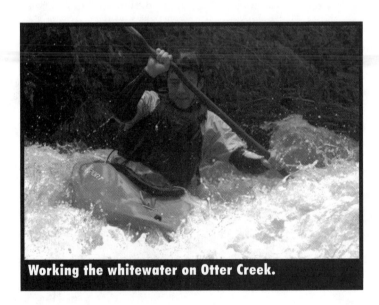

Working the whitewater on Otter Creek.

part**Five**

THE CUMBERLAND RIVER AND ITS TRIBUTARIES

POOR FORK OF THE CUMBERLAND RIVER

The Poor Fork of the Cumberland River drains Harlan and Letcher Counties in southeastern Kentucky and is the largest of the headwater streams of the North Fork of the Cumberland River. Flowing swiftly over a bed of rock and gravel, the Poor Fork winds through one of the deepest and intimate mountain valleys in eastern Kentucky. Human habitation is frequently in evidence along the Poor Fork but does surprisingly little to spoil the incredible beauty of this mountain stream. Access is excellent due to US 119 passing through the valley, which crosses the Poor Fork many times.

MAPS: Louellen, Nolansburg, Evarts, Harlan (USGS)

CUMBERLAND TO HARLAN

class	I–II
gauge	Web
level	Min. 4.5 ft. Max. flood
velocity	2.6–5.0+ (mph)
gradient	10 (fpm)
scenery	B+

DESCRIPTION: Trees envelop the stream only intermittently, allowing paddlers frequent panoramic views of the surrounding mountains with luxurious foliage and exposed rock bluffs. The banks are normally 4 to 8 feet high and gently banked. The river varies in width from 25 to 40 feet and curves leisurely through the valley. Paddling is interesting with continually changing vistas and delightful Class I and II small shoals and rapids. The Poor Fork is runnable from January through mid-April, and occasionally following heavy rains. Lateral erosion is minimal on the Poor Fork, so deadfalls are unusual. The only navigational hazards usually encountered are man-made concrete fords that cross the stream from time to time. Trips of nearly any distance are possible with the seemingly innumerable bridges over the Cumberland River on US 119.

GAUGE: The USGS gauge is Poor Fork at Cumberland, KY. Minimum reading should be 4.5 feet.

Poor Fork of the Cumberland River

KINGDOM COME STATE PARK

119 160

Ⓐ 2006

160

463 179

522

Cumberland River

510

N

215

2010

Evarts

221

KENTENIA STATE FOREST

Harlan Co.

Letcher Co.

1679

38

221

Leslie Co.

421 Harlan

Ⓑ 72

Points	River Miles	Shuttle Miles
A—B	23.5	19.0

NORTH FORK OF THE CUMBERLAND RIVER

The North Fork of the Cumberland River (often referred to as simply the Cumberland) originates near Harlan at the confluence of the Poor Fork and Catron Creek and flows west draining the east Kentucky counties of Knox, Bell, Harlan, Whitley, McCreary, and Pulaski. The run changes from Class I+ amid populated coal country, then enters the Daniel Boone National Forest, where the water becomes more challenging.

MAPS: Harlan, Wallins Creek, Balkan, Varilla, Middlesboro North, Pineville, Artemus, Barbourville, Rockholds, Saxton, Williamsburg, Wofford, Cumberland Falls, Sawyer (USGS), Daniel Boone National Forest map, South Section

HARLAN TO WEST OF PINEVILLE

class	I+
gauge	Web
level	Min. 300 Max. flood (cfs)
velocity	2.6–5.0+ (mph)
gradient	2.5 (fpm)
scenery	C

DESCRIPTION: To canoe the upper Cumberland is to become intimately acquainted with the land and the people of eastern Kentucky—their life-style and institutions are visible and alive all along the river. Although only steep, wooded hillsides meet your searching eyes, you are never out of earshot of the rumbling coal trucks or the raspy barking of a dog defending an unseen cabin in some lonely hollow.

Between Harlan and Pineville, the North Fork flows over a mud and gravel bed with infrequent small shoals and rapids (Class I+) and occasional large rocks in evidence in the stream and along the banks. From a width of approximately 50 feet at its origin, the Cumberland broadens quickly to 85–105 feet. Running west through the steep, rugged hills of the Cumberland plateau, the river winds through forest and coal country, under hanging wooden footbridges, and past the cabins of miners and the ever-present coal tipples along the railroad tracks. The Cumberland from Harlan to Pineville is frequently runnable from November through mid-May. Access is reasonably good, providing you are accustomed to steep banks.

GAUGE: The USGS gauge is Cumberland River near Harlan. Minimum reading should be 300 cfs.

North Fork of the Cumberland River
Harlan to West of Pineville

Points	River Miles	Shuttle Miles
A—B	11.44	10.98
B—C	13.59	12.3
C—D	21.45	20.02

WEST OF PINEVILLE TO WILLIAMSBURG

class	I+
gauge	Web
level	Min. 300 Max. flood (cfs)
velocity	2.6–5.0+ (mph)
gradient	2.5 (fpm)
scenery	C+

DESCRIPTION: As the Cumberland passes Pineville, it settles down into a mud bottom with steep banks, broadens a bit, and flows smoothly as it progresses through the deep valleys past Barbourville toward Williamsburg. The section from Harlan to Williamsburg is best suited to 1-day runs (pick your own) rather than canoe camping. Access point between Pineville and Williamsburg are numerous, as many bridges cross the river and allow trips of varied lengths. It is 34 miles from the put-in west of Pineville to the KY 1530 bridge, 11 miles from the KY 1530 bridge to the KY 92 bridge, and 37 miles to the Red Bird Bridge just west of Williamsburg.

GAUGE: The USGS gauge is Cumberland River near Harlan. Minimum reading should be 300 cfs.

WILLIAMSBURG TO CUMBERLAND FALLS

class	II
gauge	Web
level	Min. 400 Max. 2,000/ flood open/decked (cfs)
velocity	2.6–5.0 (mph)
gradient	2.6 (fpm)
scenery	B

DESCRIPTION: From Williamsburg to Cumberland Falls, the river flows through the Daniel Boone National Forest. Access for this section is not plentiful but is good where it exists. The Cumberland from Williamsburg to Cumberland Falls is normally runnable from November to early June.

In this section the river continues to widen until in some places it is almost 200 feet across. The gradient increases here also and some mild whitewater (Class II) is encountered, with boulders in the stream and some shoals spanning the entire width of the river. This section (beyond the mouth of Jellico Creek) is extremely remote and makes a good canoe-camping run at moderate water levels (500–1,100 cfs) and a fair whitewater run at higher levels (1,100–1,900 cfs). Rock replaces the mud bottom of the upper sections, and the current runs swift and continuously with very few pools. Boulders line the banks in increasing numbers and some flat, accessible terraces have been carved along the streamside. In the last 3 miles before reaching the KY 90 bridge, exposed rock palisades become visible on the right as the Cumberland begins to enter the deep gorge that will carry it over the falls and beyond to Lake Cumberland.

About 1 mile upstream of the falls the river curves sharply to the left, and the KY 90 bridge becomes visible downstream. Move to the right of the river for the take-out on the upstream side of the bridge (at the picnic ground and parking lot). Failure to move promptly to the right can have tragic consequences for the unlucky or inexperienced. One of the larger shoals (Class II)

North Fork of the Cumberland River West of Pineville to Williamsburg

Points	River Miles	Shuttle Miles
D—E	12.16	10.3
E—F	21.74	13.01
F—G	10.73	11.44
G—H	12.87	6.01
H—I	24.06	13.59

of this section is situated across the entire river just upstream of the take-out. If you run it on the left and fill up or capsize, you will find yourself in the main current heading for the entrance rapids to Cumberland Falls several hundred yards downstream. If you run the shoals on the right and take water or turn over, you will be in much slower current and (except at excessive levels, i.e., 1,900+ cfs) will be washed into the bank as the river narrows near

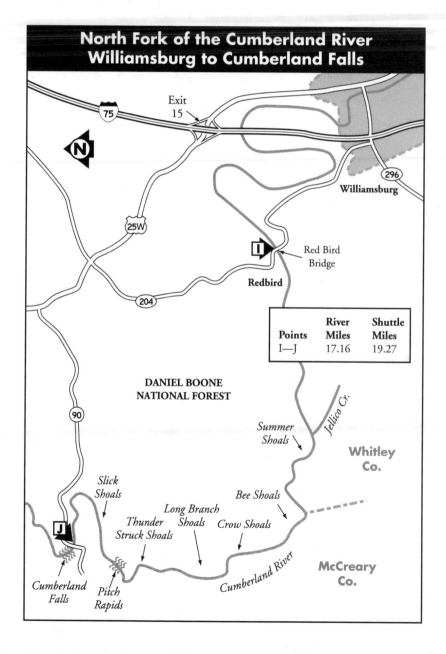

North Fork of the Cumberland River
Williamsburg to Cumberland Falls

Exit 15

Williamsburg

Red Bird Bridge

Redbird

Points	River Miles	Shuttle Miles
I—J	17.16	19.27

DANIEL BOONE NATIONAL FOREST

Jellico Cr.

Summer Shoals

Whitley Co.

Slick Shoals

Bee Shoals

Long Branch Shoals

Thunder Struck Shoals

Crow Shoals

Cumberland River

McCreary Co.

Cumberland Falls

Pitch Rapids

the bridge, or alternately swept downstream past the bridge into a huge eddy that forms along the bank near the visitors' parking lot.

ABOUT THE SHUTTLE: From Exit 15 on I-75 take US 25W North to KY 90. Turn left and take KY 90 West to Cumberland Falls State Park. To reach the put-in, return to US 25W via KY 90 and head south on 25W to KY 204. Turn right and take KY 204 South to the Redbird Bridge over the Cumberland. An access road is on the northwest side of the bridge.

GAUGE: The USGS gauge is Cumberland River at Williamsburg. A flow of 400 cfs is minimum, and 3,000 cfs is the upper runnable limit.

CUMBERLAND FALLS TO LAKE CUMBERLAND

class	III
gauge	Web
level	Min. 400 Max. 1,100/3,000 open/decked (cfs)
velocity	2.6–5.0+ (mph)
gradient	11.8 (fpm)
scenery	A

DESCRIPTION: This section of the North Fork of Cumberland is a Kentucky-protected Wild River and is one of the most popular whitewater runs in the state. Referred to as The Cumberland below the Falls by local paddlers, the river here runs through a mammoth rock gorge with boulders lining the river marking the age-old headward erosion of the falls. The run should be attempted only by experienced boaters, and extra flotation is recommended for open boats.

The run begins with a long carry from the visitors' parking lot at Cumberland Falls to a beach a quarter of a mile away at the bottom of the falls. Scenery is spectacular right from the put-in, and most paddlers take the opportunity to paddle back upstream for a truly awe-inspiring view of the falls (80 yards from the falls is as close as you can safely paddle without fighting a fantastically strong reversal current seeking to pull you into the falls).

Moving downstream, several easy Class II rapids that require no scouting are encountered before arriving at the Class III Center Rock Rapid. This rapid can be identified by the large boulders on each side that constrict the river to a channel of approximately 20 feet, and by the degree of drop that substantially exceeds that encountered previously. The rapid consists of a 25-foot-long, stairstep chute followed 50 feet later by a 3-foot vertical drop directly in front of a huge boulder that splits the current. This is Center Rock. The first drop is usually run straight down the center, and the strategy for the second is to angle the bow to the right and drop straight into the eddy on the right at the bottom of the drop. An alternate strategy for the second drop is to ride the pillow off the right side of Center Rock. It is recommended that this rapid be scouted.

Continuing downstream, the river lapses into a series of pools followed by rock gardens (at low to moderate water) and Class II rapids. The drops are small, but several of the rapids are quite technical. One of these, at about mile 4, has an undercut boulder situated in midchannel, splitting the flow. This should be run along the far right bank. Moving on, there are more long pools and small rapids. At mile 5, there is a slanting 2.5-foot drop with a playful hole at the bottom that spans the entire river. This is known as Surfing Rapid and is a delightful place to stop for lunch.

Beyond Surfing Rapid the run becomes more intense. One-half mile downstream of Surfing Rapid, the river disappears to the

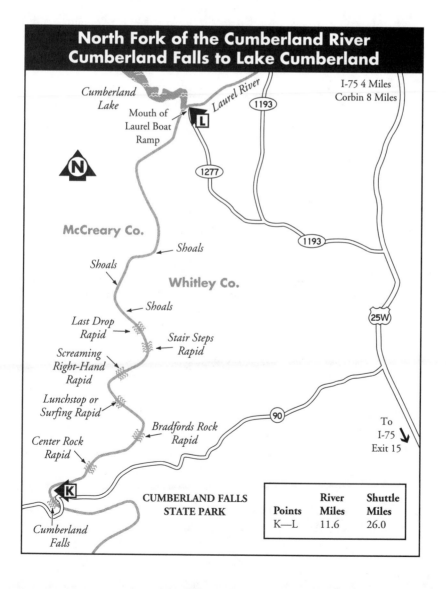

North Fork of the Cumberland River
Cumberland Falls to Lake Cumberland

Cumberland Lake

Mouth of Laurel Boat Ramp

Laurel River

1193

I-75 4 Miles
Corbin 8 Miles

L

1277

N

McCreary Co.

Shoals

Shoals

Whitley Co.

Shoals

1193

25W

Last Drop Rapid

Stair Steps Rapid

Screaming Right-Hand Rapid

Lunchstop or Surfing Rapid

Bradfords Rock Rapid

90

To I-75 Exit 15

Center Rock Rapid

K

CUMBERLAND FALLS
STATE PARK

Cumberland Falls

Points	River Miles	Shuttle Miles
K—L	11.6	26.0

right around a house-sized rock and immediately cuts left again, crashing into a boulder on the right and down a 30-foot-long chute. This intense, borderline Class III run serves up an exciting ride. Run right center and play the pillow off the boulder.

The next rapid, a quarter mile distant, is a turning 4-foot drop known as Screaming Right-Hand Rapid. At low to moderate water levels the main flow drops over a 1.5-foot ledge and splashes almost immediately on a rock that diverts the current sharply to the right over a 3-foot slanted drop. The most popular strategy here is to cut right after the first ledge, using the pillow to turn the boat. At higher water levels the river overflows the obstructing rock and a 4-foot vertical drop and a mean hydraulic is created completely across the river. Scouting is definitely required in this situation. Screaming Right-Hand Rapid becomes Class IV at higher water levels.

The next large rapid, known as Stair Steps, is a long, delightful, borderline Class III stretch that looks much worse than it is. It is easily recognized by the large hole at the top with a shark fin–shaped rock just below it. Decked boaters may want to punch the hole. For open boaters the best route is to run right of the hole and then hug the right bank all the way to the bottom. Scout on the right.

The last major rapid is appropriately named Last Drop. In this Class III area, the current winds to the right along the upstream side of a large boulder and then suddenly cuts left, dropping vertically 3 feet. Next, the current is split by a building-sized boulder in the middle of the river. Run to the right at the top, staying to the inside of the turn and away from the upstream face of the boulder. Cut hard left, taking the vertical drop as close to the boulder as possible. Go around the huge boulder that splits the current on the far right. At high water this rapid (like several others) changes drastically, forming a super-mean hole at the top. Scout (or portage) to the right.

Last Drop marks the end of the whitewater section of the Cumberland (although several small shoals are encountered farther downstream due to the low level of the lake pool). From here it is a scenic 3.5-mile paddle through the lake to the take-out at the mouth of the Laurel River on Lake Cumberland. Access is excellent at the take-out.

Dangers other than those already described include logs that occasionally become trapped in the more narrow chutes and strong headwinds while paddling off the lake.

GAUGE: The USGS gauge is Cumberland River at Williamsburg. A flow of 400 cfs is minimum, and 3,000 cfs is the upper runnable limit.

LAUREL RIVER

Spectacular scenery, great rapids, but tough to catch in its entirety at runnable levels characterizes this two-mile remnant of the Laurel River. The flow in this stretch below the U.S. Army Corps of Engineer's Laurel River Dam is controlled by the East KY Power Cooperative of Winchester (EKP), whose erratic releases can provide about two miles of fun rapids in very cold water.

MAPS: Daniel Boone National Forest, South Section map

LAUREL RIVER DAM TO LAKE CUMBERLAND

class	Class II–III (IV)
gauge	Phone
level	Min. N/A
	Max. N/A
velocity	2.6–5.0+ (mph)
gradient	30 (fpm)
scenery	A

DESCRIPTION: Predictions of releases are very difficult—even for EKP—as the dam is used to provide peak power electrical generation. Even at the height of the summer, paddlers will want to take along cold-weather boating gear, because the release water flows from the bottom of Laurel Lake and is ice cold. Though runnable year-round, the Laurel is probably best caught in August and September, when hot temperatures increase the national demand for electrical power generation. Unfortunately, due to typical summer

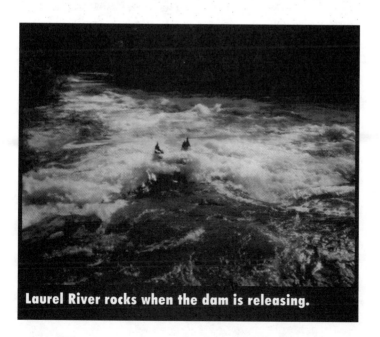

Laurel River rocks when the dam is releasing.

pool levels for Lake Cumberland, a summertime run on the Laurel could mean that the final and only Class IV rapid, Whorehouse, will be covered under the lake's stagnant flat water.

GAUGE: Flow from the Laurel Lake Dam controlled by EKP in Winchester. Highly unpredictable. Call EKP at (859) 744-4812 for flow report.

Points	River Miles	Shuttle Miles
A—B	2.1	12.5

ROCKCASTLE RIVER

The Rockcastle River originates in Laurel County and drains portions of Jackson, Rockcastle, Laurel, and Pulaski Counties. One of Kentucky's most popular rivers, the Rockcastle offers something for every type of canoeist, from Class I canoe camping to challenging Class III–IV whitewater. The scenery is appealing in this part of the Daniel Boone National Forest.

MAPS: Livingston, Bernstadt, Billows, Ano, Sawyer (USGS), Daniel Boone National Forest map, South Section

UPPER ROCKCASTLE RIVER, LIVINGSTON TO KY 1956

class	I+
gauge	Web
level	Min. 220 Max. flood (cfs)
velocity	2.6–5.0 (mph)
gradient	2.4 (fpm)
scenery	B+

DESCRIPTION: The upper sections from KY 490 to KY 1956 (old KY 80), flow over a sand and rock bed through hilly woods and farmland in the heart of the Daniel Boone National Forest. Runnable from late fall to midsummer, this section is scenic and has banks of varying steepness and some very mild (Class I+) whitewater. A favorite run for canoe campers, current is good and dangers to navigation are limited to deadfalls. An alternate access allowing a shorter day trip is under the I-75 bridge off KY 1329. Canoe rental and shuttle service is available from professional outfitters at the take-out on KY 1956.

ABOUT THE SHUTTLE: To reach the put-in from Exit 49 on I-75, take KY 909 North to US 25. Turn left and take US 25 North to KY 490 East and bridge over Rockcastle Creek in Livingston.

GAUGE: The USGS Gauge is Rockcastle River at Billows. Minimum reading should be 220 cfs.

Upper Rockcastle River

Points	River Miles	Shuttle Miles
A—B	7.3	7.0
B—C	10.6	24.0

LOWER ROCKCASTLE RIVER, KY
1956 TO CUMBERLAND RIVER LAKE

class	II (III–IV)
gauge	Web
level	Min. 220 Max. 550/ flood open/decked (cfs)
velocity	2.6–5.0+ (mph)
gradient	5.8 (fpm)
scenery	A

DESCRIPTION: The lower Rockcastle, from KY 1956 to KY 192, is a protected Kentucky Wild River and is one of Kentucky's most popular whitewater runs. The scenery is splendid with tall, forested hills along the first miles of the run giving way to high rock bluffs further downstream, with boxcar-sized boulders situated in the river and along the banks. Paddling the lower Rockcastle is both interesting and challenging. To begin with, the run used to be an exhausting 17 miles long. However, the old Howard Place offers a put-in that cuts off most of the upper Class I water that allows for runs only of the Beech Narrows.

The first 6 miles are essentially Class I with a fair current and numerous riffles and small ledges. Throughout the next 6 miles the river picks up a little gradient and several honest Class II rapids are encountered. Although these rapids are not difficult, two or three do disappear around boulders or curves. If you are not intimately familiar with the river (this or any other), you should take the time to scout these. Guidebook or no, it is not healthy to get into the habit of running rapids you cannot see the end of. The Howard Place access is around mile 11. At about mile 12 the river curves hard right and then hard left, tumbling down a Class II (III?) series of ledges and standing waves known as the Stair Steps. Beyond this rapid, the Rockcastle reverts to long pools punctuated by short Class II drops at the ends.

At about mile 15 the river appears to come to a dead end in a large boulder garden, but closer inspection reveals that whole stream is grunting laboriously between two huge rocks and falling about 4 feet. This is Beech (Creek) Narrows. Above the drop, an ill-placed boulder makes it difficult to set up. Below the drop is a very bad, highly aerated keeper hydraulic. Beyond the hydraulic the current washes directly into a large boulder. Though this Class IV rapid has been run both decked and open, we consider attempting to run it in an open boat very dangerous, with success more a function of luck (specifically, catching the rotation of the violent hydraulic on the up cycle, where it helps kick you free) than skill. A portage trail circles the boulders on the right. Our advice: carry around. If you choose to run, set up a rescue person where you are certain you can reach a person trapped in the keeper on the first throw.

Below Beech Narrows the Rockcastle assumes its normal pool and drop for another three quarters of a mile before entering a second apparent cul-de-sac. Here the river forms a large, tranquil pool before cutting hard right, churning down a fast chute, and smacking into a rock. This rapid marks the entrance to the

Lower Rockcastle River

1249

Mt. Vernon
13 miles

C

75

1956

bridge

80

80

80

1956

Exit
41

Sandy
Gap Rd.

1675

London

Acorn
Ano Rd.

Clifty Grove
Church Rd.

DANIEL BOONE
NATIONAL FOREST

Bolthouse
Ridge Rd.

1675

1003

Beech Gr.

D ← Howard Place access

1003

Stair Steps Rapid

N

Beech Narrows

Bee Rock Boat Ramp
& Campground

Lower Narrows

192

E

Cane Cr.

192

75

Pulaski Co.

Bear Gr.

192

Corbin 6 miles

Laurel Co.

1193

Boat
Ramp

Baldrock

3497

F

Rockcastle
Campground

Lake
Cumberland

Points	River Miles	Shuttle Miles
C—D	10.7	26.0
D—E	5.6	39.0
E—F	7.0	12.0

Lower Narrows, a three-quarter-mile stretch of intense and almost continuous, highly technical Class III and IV water. After the first rapid of the Lower Narrows (which is followed by a 200-yard pool), the remaining four rapids are lined up literally one behind the other in an amazing stretch of tumbling, turbulent whitewater that lambastes the paddler with every challenge in the book. There are, thankfully however, some large eddies that let an embattled paddler stop after each rapid to bail, collect wits, and scramble up the banks to scout whatever lurks ahead.

The rapids of the Lower Narrows are all runnable, but they demand considerable expertise in water reading and whitewater tactics. They also demand considerable time. The whole narrows is a series of twisting, turning, blind drops so that it is impossible to see what lies beyond the next ledge. Thus, each rapid must be scouted individually. This entails a seemingly endless routine of jumping in and out of boats and scrambling up immense boulders to sneak a look at the next rapid. The scouting and the boulder hopping are necessary, of course, but also time-consuming. A good running time for the Lower Narrows by an experienced group of four open-canoe tandem teams would be about two hours. The alternative to running the Narrows is carrying via a trail on the east bank that is reached by climbing the bank at the end of the pool marking the entrance to the first rapid. In running the Lower Rockcastle, time is always a prime consideration. Therefore, whitewater enthusiasts will want to start at Howard Place, running the Narrows at their leisure.

Beyond the Lower Narrows there are a Class II and a borderline Class III stretch that are blind turns and should be scouted. The first rapid (the Class II) particularly has a tendency to trap floating logs in the spring. Downstream from the Class III it is approximately 1 mile to the take-out at Bee Rock Boat Ramp.

As you might gather, the Rockcastle River is beautiful, challenging, and exhausting if this entire section is run in a single day. The paddler has more than put in a full day before even reaching the most demanding part of the run. An early put-in (10 a.m. at the absolute latest) is a necessity. Only paddlers with a lot of experience on technical rivers should attempt the Lower Narrows. Extra flotation is a must for open canoes. Dangers other than those already mentioned include deadfalls on several turns along the first 12 miles Access is good at both put-in and take-out. Average stream width is 40–60 feet A much calmer paddle can be enjoyed by all on Lake Cumberland, for 7 miles from Bee Rock to the Rockcastle Campground boat ramp off KY 1193.

SHUTTLE: To reach the take-out from Exit 38 on I-75 near London, head west on KY 192 for 18 miles to the bridge over the Rockcastle River. The Bee Rock Boat Ramp is on the east side of the river. To reach the put-in from Exit 41 on I-75, take KY 80 West to KY 1956. Turn right on KY 1956 and follow it west to bridge over Rockcastle on outfitter on left before river. To reach the Howard Place access from Exit 41 on I-75, take KY 80 West to Sandy Gap Rd., on the west side of the KY 80 bridge over the Rockcastle. Turn left on Sandy Gap Rd. and follow it to KY 1675. Turn left onto KY 1675 and follow it to Acorn Ano Rd. Turn left on Acorn Ano Rd. and follow it to Bolthouse Ridge Rd. Turn right on Bolthouse Ridge Rd., which passes through reclaimed strip-mine land. Follow Bolthouse Ridge Rd. as it descends to the Rockcastle and Lick Creek, about 2 miles above Beech Creek. A four-wheel-drive vehicle with high ground clearance is wise on the lower part of Bolthouse Rd., especially after rains.

GAUGE: The USGS Gauge is Rockcastle River at Billows. The minimum reading should be 220 cfs.

BUCK CREEK

Buck Creek is a small, scenic, Class II whitewater stream that drains the eastern half of Pulaski County. Several small caves along the run provide the opportunity for interesting side trips. Runnable from KY 1677 to KY 192 following periods of heavy rain, Buck Creek winds through forested hillsides with some exposed rock visible, especially in the lower sections below KY 80.

MAPS: Shopville, Dykes (USGS)

KY 1677 TO KY 192

class	I–II
gauge	Visual
level	Min. 200
	Max. flood
	(cfs)
velocity	2.6–5.0+
	(mph)
gradient	3.5 (fpm)
scenery	B

DESCRIPTION: The level of difficulty on Buck Creek is easy Class II with most rapids consisting of very small ledges or small standing waves. Route selection is obvious, and no scouting is required. Deadfalls constitute the primary hazard to navigation. The average stream width is 35–45 feet Access is good, including the KY 1003 bridge. Water levels on Buck Creek are usually optimal when surrounding larger streams (the Rockcastle River and the North Fork of the Cumberland River) are high or marginally flooded. The run can be extended below KY 192 to Lake Cumberland at KY 769 (reached from Somerset). However, most of these final 11.5 miles are on the slack pool of the lake.

SHUTTLE: To reach the put-in from Somerset, take KY 80 East to KY 461. Turn left on KY 461 and follow it to KY 1677. Turn right on KY 1677 and follow it to Rainey Rd., just before bridge over Buck Creek. Turn right on Rainey Rd. and reach access on left. To reach the lower access from Somerset, take KY 80 East to KY 914. Turn right on KY 914 and follow it to KY 192. Turn left on KY 192 and travel east to bridge over Buck Creek.

GAUGE: Buck Creek is a look-and-see proposition. However, a good guesstimate can be made for running Buck Creek by checking the USGS gauge for Rockcastle River at Billows. The minimum reading should be 600 cfs.

Buck Creek

N

A

461 bridge

B

1677

Rainey Rd.

80

C

1003

80

Somerset 4 miles

1675

Bent

D

DANIEL BOONE NATIONAL FOREST

Randall Chapel

1003

192

bridge

E

1675

Buck Cr.

769

192

1643

1097

F

Points	River Miles	Shuttle Miles
A—B	3.15	3.86
B—C	5.72	5.08
C—D	8.87	6.45
D—E	4.86	7.29
E—F	11.44	9.30

Cumberland River

BIG SOUTH FORK GORGE OF
THE CUMBERLAND RIVER (TENNESSEE)

The Big South Fork Gorge is part of the headwaters of the Big South Fork of the Cumberland River. Although situated entirely in Tennessee, it is worth including in this guide because it is a very popular whitewater run enjoyed by advanced Kentucky paddlers. Consisting of almost continuous Class III (and IV?) whitewater, the run begins on the Clear Fork (which combines with New River of Tennessee to form the Big South Fork of the Cumberland River) about 12 miles southwest of Oneida and ends at Leatherwood Ford, west of Oneida.

MAPS: Oneida South, Honey Creek (USGS), BSFNRRA map

BURNT MILL BRIDGE TO LEATHERWOOD FORD

class	III–IV
gauge	Web
level	Min. 450 Max. 6,000 (cfs)
velocity	2.6–5.0+ (mph)
gradient	19.5 (fpm)
scenery	A+

DESCRIPTION: In all, there are 13 major rapids and several dozen smaller ones in the Big South Fork Gorge. Considered by many to be a decked-boat and rafting river, the Big South Fork Gorge is run successfully on by both solo and tandem open-boaters. The nature of the run varies incredibly with water level, being extremely technical at lower water and big and pushy (much like the New River Gorge in West Virginia) when flowing high. At moderate levels, paddlers get a taste of both worlds with quick, technical water on the Clear Fork and bigger, less technical water below the confluence (of the Clear Fork and the New River). Scenery is magnificent, when you have time to notice it, with boulders lining the banks and canyon walls rising on both sides. For a Class III (IV) river, the Big South Fork Gorge is mostly free of dangers; deadfalls and logjams are infrequent, and the holes are washouts at almost all levels. However, watch out for undercut rocks that have resulted in close calls in the past. The drops, however, are sizable (several exceeding 4 feet), and helmets are a must for all paddlers. Also, some of the rapids are extremely long, making rescue difficult (especially at higher water levels). Extra flotation is essential for open canoes, and a good roll is definitely recommended for decked boaters. Access at the river is good at both put-in and take-out. The Big South Fork Gorge is runnable from late fall to mid-May in years of average rainfall.

GAUGE: The USGS gauge is South Fork Cumberland River at Leatherwood Ford, TN. The minimum level is 450 cfs; maximum level is 6,000 cfs.

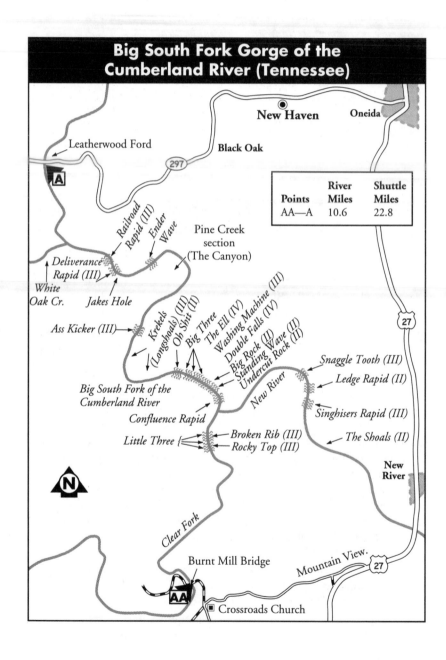

Big South Fork Gorge of the Cumberland River (Tennessee)

New Haven   Oneida

Leatherwood Ford   Black Oak

297

A

Points	River Miles	Shuttle Miles
AA—A	10.6	22.8

Railroad Rapid (III)   *Ender Wave*   Pine Creek section (The Canyon)

Deliverance Rapid (III)

White Oak Cr.   Jakes Hole

Krekels (Longshoals) (II)   *Oh Shit (II)*   *Big Three*   *The Ell (IV)*   *Washing Machine (III)*   *Double Falls (IV)*   *Big Rock (II)*   *Standing Wave (II)*   *Undercut Rock (II)*

Ass Kicker (III)

27

Snaggle Tooth (III)

Ledge Rapid (II)

Big South Fork of the Cumberland River

New River

Confluence Rapid

Singhisers Rapid (III)

Little Three {   — *Broken Rib (III)*   — *Rocky Top (III)*   — *The Shoals (II)*

New River

N

Clear Fork

Burnt Mill Bridge   Mountain View.

27

AA

▣ Crossroads Church

BIG SOUTH FORK OF THE CUMBERLAND RIVER (KENTUCKY)

Flowing out of Scott County (TN), the Big South Fork of the Cumberland River flows north through McCreary County (KY) before emptying into Lake Cumberland. One of the most popular canoe camping runs in the southeastern United States, the Big South Fork winds through the wooded bluffs and ridges of the Big South Fork National River and Recreation Area (BSFNRRA). An exceptionally beautiful river flowing swiftly below stately exposed rock pinnacles, the Big South Fork is dotted with huge boulders midstream and along the banks and padded along either side by steep hillsides of hardwoods and evergreens. Wildflowers brighten the vista in the spring, and wildlife is plentiful.

MAPS: Oneida South, Oneida North, Barthell, Nevelsville, Burnsville (USGS), BSFNRRA map

LEATHERWOOD FORD TO KY 927

class	II (IV)
gauge	Web
level	Min. 200 Max. 1,300/3,000 open/decked (cfs)
velocity	2.6–5.0 (5.0+) (mph)
gradient	10 (fpm)
scenery	A+

DESCRIPTION: Not only will the beauty capture your attention, but the paddling is interesting with as many as five legitimate (and six borderline) Class II rapids (some of them quite long) consisting primarily of nontechnical small ledges and standing waves. The main channel is easily discerned in these rapids, and scouting is normally not required. At moderate to low water, all the Class II rapids can be run with a loaded boat. At higher water, loaded open boats can avail themselves of sneak routes to avoid swamping. The rapids are broken by occasional long, slow stretches.

Two Class III–IV rapids are encountered on this section of the Big South Fork. Both are technical, complex, high-velocity chutes that are dangerous at certain water levels. The first is Angel Falls, 1.5 miles into the run, where the river takes an 8-foot drop in closely spaced 1- and 2-foot increments with the main flow being forced between two large rocks toward the right of the river. After the first two ledges (normally run from the left), converging smaller chutes of water join the main flow from the right, further aerating the water and causing the current to impact a large boulder to the left. A smaller boulder at the bottom of the rapid, in conjunction with the converging currents from the right, causes the current o turn left at the end of the rapid before pooling out. This rapid must be scouted, and different strategies are appropriate at different water levels (though as a point of departure Angel Falls is usually run far left to left center to right center). Regardless of water level, boats should be emptied of all gear before attempting the run. Portage is possible via a trail on the right 50 yards upstream of the rapid and is strongly recommended at all water levels except for competent, very experienced boaters.

The Devil's Jump, a Class IV rapid, is closer to the end of the run, just upstream of the Blue Heron Mine. Here the current flows into a house-sized boulder from whence it is diverted at an angle through a high-velocity chute. The trick is to align your boat for the chute by riding the pillow off the left of the boulder. This is done at low to moderate water levels by practically setting your bow on a collision course for the giant boulder and then allowing the pillow to divert your bow into the top of the chute. The route to the right of the giant boulder is usually avoided because of a mean hydraulic at the bottom. Once again, all boats should be run without gear and after careful scouting (if you do not understand the dynamics of converging currents, leave this rapid alone). Portage is possible upstream and to the left of the rapid and is recommended at all water levels except for competent, experienced boaters.

The Big South Fork is runnable year-round in this section, except for fall in dry years. Day trips can be made from Leatherwood Ford to Station Camp and using other combinations of access points. However, several nice camping locations are available along the run (which can be lengthened to 3 or more days by continuing on down into Lake Cumberland). It is 27 miles from Leatherwood Ford to Blue Heron, 4.8 more to Yamacraw, 7.4 more to Alum Ford, and another 11.5 to the boat ramp near Nevelsville. Between Leatherwood and Devil's Jump, the river averages 80–110 feet but sometimes broadens to as much as 150 feet Below Devil's Jump, the Big South Fork widens to an average of 115–150 feet and settles down conspicuously with fewer rapids in evidence. Downstream from Yamacraw, the current comes to a halt as it reaches the lake pool. Dangers to navigation are as described, plus a damaged concrete ford between Blue Heron and Yamacraw that must be portaged on the right, and the potential of the river to rise at an alarming rate after heavy rains (remember this when you set up camp). Because of the remoteness of the Big South Fork, access points are few and far between and connected by narrow roads.

GAUGE: The USGS Gauge is South Fork Cumberland River at Leatherwood Ford, TN. The minimum level is 200 cfs, anything below that and you will be scraping in places. The maximum level is 3,000 cfs.

Big South Fork of the Cumberland River (Kentucky)

D
Little South Fork of the Cumberland River
Nevelsville 927

27

Alum Ford Campground, boat access & road access

700

N

C Hilltop

DANIEL BOONE NATIONAL FOREST

Yamacraw

701

791

92

Whitley City

Blue Heron Campground

Blue Heron

742

B

Devils Jump
Berthas Bump

Points	River Miles	Shuttle Miles
A—B	23.0	40.0
B—C	4.8	7.3
C—D	14.8	28.0

McCreary Co. Kentucky

Scott Co. Tennessee

Big Island

Angel Falls

New Haven

297
297

Oneida

27

A
Leatherwood Ford

LITTLE SOUTH FORK OF THE CUMBERLAND RIVER

The Little South Fork of the Cumberland River is a Kentucky Wild River. Little used by paddlers due to its seasonal nature and its remoteness, it is nevertheless one of the most beautiful of Kentucky's rivers. Above all, the Little South Fork is amazingly pristine and rugged. Draining the eastern portion of Wayne County and the western portion of McCreary County before emptying into the Big South Fork of the Cumberland River, the Little South Fork runs cool and clear over a rock and mud bottom through steep, wooded hills.

MAPS: Bell Farm, Coopersville, Nevelsville (USGS)

PARMLEYSVILLE TO BIG SOUTH FORK

class	I–II
gauge	Visual
level	Min. 200
	Max. flood
	(cfs)
velocity	2.6–5.0
	(mph)
gradient	3.6 (fpm)
scenery	A+

DESCRIPTION: This truly beautiful water course is runnable from November through mid-May downstream from Parmleysville. The stream is primarily Class I with some small shoals and rapids that approach Class II. The river is 30 feet wide in the upstream sections and does not broaden beyond 60 feet as it flows toward its mouth. Access is difficult from all but one or two bridges, and shuttles are long, particularly for the shuttle between the lower river and KY 927, on the Big South Fork. However, the Parmleysville put-in is easy at a low-water bridge. It is a 14.5-miles run between Parmleysville and the KY 92 bridge (access for KY 92 is on west side of bridge). Exposed rock and a variety of hardwoods grace the usually steep riverbank along with the common proliferation of willows upstream of KY 92. Downstream of KY 92, near Freedom Chapel, the stream enters a massive and beautiful vertical rock-wall gorge. Dangers to navigation include deadfalls and flash flood potential.

ABOUT THE SHUTTLE: From US 27 in Whitley City, take US 27 North to KY 927. Turn left on KY 927 and follow it 9 miles to dead end at a boat ramp on the Big South Fork near Nevelsville. To reach the uppermost access, take KY 92 West from Whitley City to KY 1756, passing over the Little South

Fork on a bridge en route. Turn left on KY 1756 and follow it to veer right on Parmleysville Road. After climbing and descending a big hill, look left for an unnamed gravel road leading left to a low-water bridge over the Little South Fork.

GAUGE: Check the Little South Fork when the nearby Big South Fork is running high and muddy.

ROCK CREEK

Rock Creek is a small, beautiful, and threatened creek that drains the southwestern corner of McCreary County near the Tennessee border. The upper section of the creek, above White Oak junction, is protected as a Kentucky Wild River. Unfortunately for paddlers, however, the only canoeable section is from below White Oak junction, where coal mining discharge pollutes the water. Rock Creek runs through the steep, wooded hillsides of the Daniel Boone National Forest. Banks on the road side of the stream vary in steepness, and the far bank often approaches being vertical. The streamside is dense with scrub vegetation and some trees, with deadfalls not unusual in the upper sections.

MAPS: Barthell SW, Bell Farm, Barthell (USGS), BSFNRRA map, Daniel Boone National Forest map, South Section

WHITE OAK JUNCTION TO BIG SOUTH FORK

class	II–III (IV)
gauge	Visual
level	Min. 195 Max. 350/ 400 open/decked (cfs)
velocity	5.0+ (mph)
gradient	15 (fpm)
scenery	B+

DESCRIPTION: Runnable in the spring and following heavy rain, Rock Creek is a Class II–III, whitewater run with numerous small ledges and a variety of boulders and rocks. Access is easy with White Oak Road, KY 1363 running along the stream. The logical put-in is at the bridge at Devil's Creek Road with a take-out on the Big South Fork of the Cumberland near Yamacraw. Above Devil's Creek Road, Rock Creek is runnable in spots but would require excessive flow for an unobstructed run. At one spot a half-mile upstream of Devil's Creek, the entire stream pools and drops over a ledge to the left under an undercut rock that makes portaging necessary at any water level. For the most part the stream is strewn with boulders and approximately 25–40 feet in width.

GAUGE: The entire run can be scouted from KY 1363. If the Big South Fork is running well above normal flows following heavy rains, consider Rock Creek.

Rock Creek

Whitley
City

27

92

701

700

Big South Fork

Yamacraw

Cumberland River

C

Yamacraw →
Bridge

1363   Bridge

B

92

Devils Creek Rd.

Bridge

A

Rock Cr.

White Oak
Junction

1363

White Oak Rd.

N

DANIEL BOONE
NATIONAL FOREST

1363

Points	River Miles	Shuttle Miles
A—B	2.86	2.86
B—C	2.63	2.63

CUMBERLAND RIVER

After passing through the Wolf Creek Dam in Russell County, the Cumberland River turns south through Cumberland and Monroe Counties before crossing once more into Tennessee. This tailwater was created in 1952 with the completion of Wolf Creek Dam. Interestingly, the water discharging from the dam averages 52°F. Compared with other Kentucky rivers of similar size, it is remarkably free of powerboat traffic.

MAPS: Wolf Creek Dam, Burkesville, Waterview, Blacks Ferry, Vernon, Celina (USGS)

WOLF CREEK DAM TO TENNESSEE

class	I
gauge	Phone
level	Min. 300 Max. flood (cfs)
velocity	0–2.5 (2.6–5.0) (mph)
gradient	0.6 (fpm)
scenery	B

DESCRIPTION: Coming cool and clear out of Wolf Creek Dam, the Cumberland is runnable all year here. Flow from the dam dictates river speed. Averaging 200–400 feet in width, access is easy and there are few dangers. Trips of varied lengths are easily made with numerous access points, including a riverside launch on Lower River Road in Burkesville. Although this section of the Cumberland lacks the wilderness quality of the Big South Fork, it nevertheless flows through beautiful, steep woodland and farm country. Mud banks rise on the average 6–12 feet to a floodplain that varies in width and is lined with tall grass and willows. Wind and a few boats are the only hazards to navigation.

GAUGE: The Cumberland is runnable all year. However, the flow rates can vary with the dam release schedule. For the release schedule, call the Wolf Creek Dam Hotline at (800) 238-2264, then dial 4, and then 34.

Cumberland River
Wolf Creek Dam to Tennessee

Points	River Miles	Shuttle Miles
A—B	17.88	20.74
B—C	14.3	15.73
C—D	5.72	5.43
D—E	2.86	3.29
E—F	4.58	3.72
F—G	14.16	16.45
G—H	10.01	10.5
H—I	7.87	8.58

partSix

THE SALT RIVER SYSTEM OF THE WESTERN BLUEGRASS

SALT RIVER

Originating in Boyle County near Danville, the Salt River flows north and then west, draining the Bluegrass counties of Mercer, Anderson, Spencer, and Bullitt before disappearing into the Fort Knox Military Reservation en route to emptying into the Ohio River near West Point. Runnable downstream of KY 1160 to Taylorsville Lake from late fall to late spring and downstream of Taylorsville Lake almost all year, the Salt is a winding, sycamore-lined stream often bordered by medium-sized hills and ridges on one bank and broad fields or grazing land on the other. Current is usually swift, particularly in the winter and spring; access is generally good. The Salt cannot be paddled into the Fort Knox Military Reservation; therefore all runs must end at Shepherdsville.

MAPS: Cornishville, McBrayer, Lawrenceburg, Glensboro, Ashbrook, Chaplin, Bloomfield, Taylorsville, Waterford, Mt. Washington, Brooks, Shepherdsville (USGS)

KY 1160 BRIDGE TO GLENSBORO

class	I+
gauge	Web
level	Min. 200 Max. flood (cfs)
velocity	2.6–5.0 (mph)
gradient	2.0 (fpm)
scenery	B–

DESCRIPTION: Running over a bottom of sandy mud, the Salt is dotted with dozens of small islands. Banks in the upper sections incline gently but below Taylorsville become increasingly steep and muddy. The level of difficulty is Class I+ in most sections with some tight maneuvering occasionally required to navigate around the islands. Deadfalls and logjams are numerous and constitute the primary hazards to paddlers. (There is also a 5-foot dam at McBrayer that must be portaged.) Frequent small rapids, ledges, and waves liven up the paddling but should pose no problems. It is 19 miles from the KY 1160 bridge to McBrayer, and 18 miles from McBrayer to Glensboro.

GAUGE: The USGS gauge is Salt River at Glensboro, KY. Minimum reading should be 200 cfs.

Points	River Miles	Shuttle Miles
A—B	1.43	4.43
B—C	4.58	3.86
C—D	2.57	4.29
D—E	6.29	4.15
E—F	4.5	6.29
F—G	3.93	1.64
G—H	5.01	2.86
H—I	3.02	4.0
I—J	3.15	4.43
J—K	2.86	2.72

TAYLORSVILLE DAM TO SHEPHERDSVILLE

class	I
gauge	Web
level	Min 220 Max. flood (cfs)
velocity	0–2.5 (mph)
gradient	1.9 (fpm)
scenery	B–

DESCRIPTION: The Salt averages 55–75 feet wide below Taylorsville. It is 5 miles from the dam to Taylorsville, 22 miles from Taylorsville to US 31E, and 15 miles from US 31E to Shepherdsville. Paddlers must take out before reaching Fort Knox.

GAUGE: The USGS gauge is Salt River at Shepherdsville. The minimum reading should be 220 cfs.

Salt River
Taylorsville Dam to Shepherdsville

N

Taylorsville Lake

Spencer Co.

Nelson Co.

44

2239

Salt River

N

55

Taylorsville

55

44

652

1392

652

Spencer Co.

1251

2285

48

Plum Creek

623 Old Waterford Rd.

1060

O

Waterford

44

31E

P

Bullitt Co.

Jefferson Co.

Mount Washington

480

Q

1442

Nelson Co.

Bullitt Co.

Lawson Ln.

1604

44

1442

245

1526

61

480

65

65

61

1020
access
behind school

Exit 117

2237

44

R

Shepherdsville

Points	River Miles	Shuttle Miles
N—O	14.44	7.29
O—P	7.44	12.87
P—Q	4.15	3.86
Q—R	11.44	10.73

PLUM CREEK

Plum Creek originates in southwestern Shelby County and flows south through Spencer County before emptying into the Salt River west of Taylorsville. Only runnable after heavy rains, the Plum roller-coasters over a seemingly continuous series of ledges ranging from several inches to three feet in height.

MAPS: Fisherville, Waterford (USGS)

WILSONVILLE TO WATERFORD

class	II (III)
gauge	Visual
level	Min. 2.5 ft. Max. flood
velocity	5.0+ (mph)
gradient	25.7 (fpm)
scenery	C

DESCRIPTION: Flowing over a rock bed between high, well-defined banks of varying steepness, Plum Creek is unique among high-water streams (that is, streams that can only be run after exceptionally heavy rains). First, there are practically no deadfalls and the channel is almost uniformly unobstructed. Second, the geology of the riverbed limits lateral erosion and keeps the stream neatly within the confines of its banks even at very high levels.

Plum Creek can be run from the Hochstrasser Road at the Shelby–Spencer County line all the way to its mouth at the Salt River. Above KY 155, however, numerous fences spanning the stream make paddling both dangerous and bothersome. Below KY 155 about a third of a mile is a low-water bridge. Beyond this point the river is normally clear of strainers (man-made or otherwise).

The run is a good, solid Class II with an average gradient of 25 feet per mile and would have to be upgraded to Class III at higher water levels (above 3 feet on the gauge on the upstream side of the KY 3192 bridge). The whitewater is challenging but not particularly technical, consisting of nearly continuous waves, small holes, and lots of vertical drops. At higher levels, eddies are few and far between. There are several major rapids between the KY 1319 bridge and the KY 44 bridge that can be easily scouted from KY 1060, which runs parallel to the stream. The principal attraction of Plum Creek is its whitewater and proximity to Louisville (35 miles). Scenery along the creek is only passable at best, with habitation all along its banks and less-than-average vegetation. Surrounding countryside consists of rolling terrain spotted with small farms. Dangers to navigation include several low-water fords and small dams. Because the nature (and difficulty) of the run varies markedly at different water levels, thorough scouting is advised.

GAUGE: The gauge is on the KY 3192 bridge at upper Plum Creek. The gauge should be at least 2.5 feet.

Plum Creek

Points	River Miles	Shuttle Miles
A—B	3.6	3.5
B—C	5.3	5.2

FLOYDS FORK OF THE SALT RIVER

A main tributary of the Salt River, Floyds Fork flows southwest along the Oldham–Shelby County line, across western Jefferson County, and into Bullitt County, where it joins the Salt River near Shepherdsville. Access is good, especially in Jefferson and Shelby Counties, where the banks are not particularly steep.

MAPS: Crestwood, Fisherville, Jeffersontown, Mt. Washington (USGS)

KY 1408 BRIDGE TO US 31E BRIDGE

class	I+
gauge	Web
level	Min. 200 Max. flood (cfs)
velocity	2.6–5.0 (mph)
gradient	4.5 (fpm
scenery	B–

DESCRIPTION: Runnable downstream of KY 1408 from midfall through the spring, Floyds Fork rolls alternately beneath steep hills and ridges and fields and pastureland. Current is swift, and the stream is punctuated with small ledges, shoals, and many brush islands. The river averages 35–55 feet in width. The stream's level of difficulty is Class I+, with good paddling techniques necessary to navigate around many of the islands. Dangers to navigation include numerous deadfalls and logjams.

GAUGE: The USGS gauge is Floyds Fork at Fisherville, KY. Minimum reading should be 200 cfs.

US 31E BRIDGE TO SALT RIVER IN SHEPHERDSVILLE

class	I+
gauge	Web
level	Min. 200 Max. flood (cfs)
velocity	2.6–5.0 (mph)
gradient	3.9 (fpm)
scenery	B–

DESCRIPTION: The river broadens, averaging 45–65 feet wide. It is 12 miles from the US 31E bridge to the KY 1526 bridge and 11.5 miles farther to the access point in Shepherdsville, which is on the main Salt River.

Floyds Fork of the Salt River
KY 1408 Bridge to US 31E Bridge

Points	River Miles	Shuttle Miles
A—B	6.58	5.01
B—C	3.00	2.86
C—D	2.15	3.58
D—E	6.44	5.72
E—F	1.43	1.57
F—G	1.72	1.29
G—H	7.15	7.44
H—I	2.86	4.15
I—J	0.72	1.14
J—K	2.29	4.43

GAUGE: The USGS gauge is Floyds Fork at Fisherville, KY. Minimum reading should be 200 cfs.

Floyds Fork of the Salt River
US 31E Bridge to Salt River in Shepherdsville

Points	River Miles	Shuttle Miles
K—L	11.73	10.87
L—M	7.87	6.72
M—N	2.86	2.43

ROLLING FORK OF THE SALT RIVER

Flowing northwest out of Casey County, the Rolling Fork of the Salt River drains portions of Marion, Larue, Nelson, Bullitt, and Hardin Counties before joining the Salt River deep inside the Fort Knox Military Reservation. Running over a mud and rock bottom and between wall-like mud banks carved by lateral erosion, the Rolling Fork is runnable downstream of the US 68 bridge from November to May. Be warned that floating the Rolling Fork through Fort Knox is strictly prohibited.

MAPS: Lebanon West, Raywick, Howardstown, New Haven, Nelsonville, Lebanon Junction (USGS)

KY 68 Bridge near Lebanon to Lebanon Junction

class	I+
gauge	Web
level	Min. 200 Max. flood (cfs)
velocity	2.6–5.0 (mph)
gradient	2.2 (fpm)
scenery	B–C

DESCRIPTION: Largely, the Rolling Fork meanders beside broad fields on one side of the stream and rolling hills (usually grazing land) on the other. Above the mud walls that contain the river, the banks are brushy and tree-lined. Grass and brush islands are common in the stream. The most scenic section of the Rolling Fork is between the Marion County line and New Haven (in Nelson County), where the river temporarily departs the farm plains and winds beneath the tall, rugged knobs (a "knob" is larger than a big hill and smaller than a mountain and is so named because of characteristically steep sides and rounded top) of southern Nelson and northern Larue Counties. In this area the precipitous hillsides are densely forested, and some exposed rock is visible both in the river gorge and high on the ridges. Emerging from the knobs near New Haven, the Rolling Fork continues through hilly farmland until it disappears among the wooded, rolling hills of Fort Knox. The abundance of farmland can stain the Rolling Fork after prolonged rains. Its level of difficulty is Class I+ between US 68 and the Lebanon Junction. Access points are numerous, allowing runs of varying lengths. Navigational dangers are limited to deadfalls, logjams, and several brush islands that necessitate good boat control. The Rolling Fork enters Fort Knox Military Reservation shortly beyond Lebanon Junction. Paddling through the reservation has been prohibited since the September 11, 2001 terrorist attacks. It is 18 miles from the US 68 bridge to Raywick, 17 miles from Raywick to the KY 84 bridge, 18 miles from the KY 84 bridge to New Haven, and 29 miles from New Haven to Lebanon Junction.

GAUGE: The USGS gauge is Rolling Fork near Boston. The minimum reading should be 200 cfs.

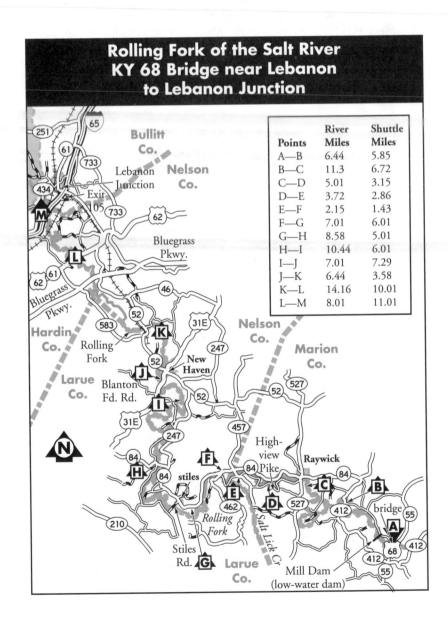

Rolling Fork of the Salt River
KY 68 Bridge near Lebanon
to Lebanon Junction

Points	River Miles	Shuttle Miles
A—B	6.44	5.85
B—C	11.3	6.72
C—D	5.01	3.15
D—E	3.72	2.86
E—F	2.15	1.43
F—G	7.01	6.01
G—H	8.58	5.01
H—I	10.44	6.01
I—J	7.01	7.29
J—K	6.44	3.58
K—L	14.16	10.01
L—M	8.01	11.01

BEECH FORK OF THE ROLLING FORK
OF THE SALT RIVER

Beech Fork originates in eastern Marion County, flows northwest into Washington County, where it joins the Chaplin River, and then turns southwest through Nelson County before finally emptying into the Rolling Fork of the Salt River near Boston, Kentucky.

MAPS: Bardstown, Cravens, Lebanon Junction (USGS)

KY 49 TO BOSTON

class	I (III+)
gauge	Web
level	Min. 200
	Max. flood
	(cfs)
velocity	2.6–5.0
	(mph)
gradient	1.4 (fpm)
scenery	C+

DESCRIPTION: An extremely winding river, the Beech Fork is runnable from November to early June from KY 49 to its mouth. Tree-lined and having mud banks of varying steepness while flowing over a mud bottom, the Beech Fork (in its runnable section) snakes through the modest knobs of central Nelson County, past the distilleries on the southern edge of Bardstown, and on to the broad, gently rolling farm plains of Boston. Its level of difficulty is Class I with the exception of a man-made Class III+ (a collapsed boulder dam) one-quarter of a mile upstream of the US 31E bridge. The overall drop here is about 5 feet. This rapid can be safely run but changes incredibly with varying water levels and should always be scouted. The rapid is dominated by a vault-sized boulder right in the middle of the river at the bottom of a 4-foot drop. To its left (as you look downstream) is a mean hole, particularly at higher water levels. When the water is up, there is a nice route on the far left; otherwise, choose your own poison or carry around. Other hazards to navigation include numerous brush islands, deadfalls, and some logjams. A good day trip extends 8 miles from KY 49 to Bardstown and the 31E bridge.

GAUGE: The USGS gauge is Beech Fork at Bardstown. The minimum reading should be 200 cfs.

Beech Fork of the Rolling Fork of the Salt River

Bluegrass Pkwy.

150

62

man-made rapids

31E 150

bridge

49

2735

A

Bardstown

B

31E

46

245

31E

733

Points	River Miles	Shuttle Miles
A—B	7.79	5.86
B—C	21.59	15.02
C—D	2.86	3.15

62

733

Beech Fork

46

52

733

52

Rolling Fork

C

Raywick

Bluegrass Pkwy.

D

N

part**Seven**

HEADWATERS OF THE GREEN RIVER

GREEN RIVER

The Green River is one of Kentucky's largest, longest, and most navigable rivers. Originating in southwestern Lincoln County, the Green River flows west, creating Green River Lake and draining 12 counties before emptying into the Ohio River across from Evansville, Indiana. Although most of the Green River is canoeable all year, certain sections are far more inviting than others. For this reason, the river has been divided into sections. (The lower Green River, from Houchins Ferry at Livermore to the mouth of the Green River at the Rough River, is found in Part Eight, Streams of the Western Coal Fields.)

MAPS: Liberty, Phil, Dunnville, Knifely, Cane Valley, Gresham, Greensburg, Summersville, Hudgins, Center, Canmer, Munfordville, Cub Run, Mammoth Cave (USGS), Mammoth Cave National Park map, Green River Lake Army Corps of Engineers map

LIBERTY TO GREEN RIVER LAKE

class	I+
gauge	Visual
level	Min. 220 Max. flood (cfs)
velocity	2.6–5.0 (mph)
gradient	3.8 (fpm)
scenery	B

DESCRIPTION: This upper section of the Green is not often paddled but is very pleasant. Running through farmland and along some steep, wooded hills, the river is tree-lined and flows swiftly. Banks are of mud and vary in steepness. At low water, sandbars and brush islands are common. Although farms line the floodplain, the river itself is fairly secluded, and signs of human habitation are surprisingly few. Some modest but interesting exposed rock formations combine with rippling, playful Class I+ water to keep the paddling interesting. Access is good in most places, and navigational hazards are limited to deadfalls and occasional logjams. This section is runnable from November through mid-June. It is 15 miles from Liberty to KY 1640 and 9 miles from KY 1640 to Neatsville. Private property limits

Green River
Liberty to Green River Lake

To Danville
25 miles

70

127

A Liberty

70

127

B

River
Valley Rd.

C

1640

127

2310

Casey Co.

Adair Co.

Russell
Co.

206

Eunice

Neatsville

D

2289

76

Campbellsville
18 miles

551

Holmes Bend
Boat Dock

E

F

Asher Holmes Rd.

*Green
River Lake*

2971

Holmes
Bend Rd.

Louie B.
Nunn Pkwy.
6 miles

N

Points	River Miles	Shuttle Miles
A—B	9.22	6.44
B—C	6.08	5.72
C—D	8.58	10.0
D—E	13.2	12.51
E—F	5.36	6.86

canoe-camping possibilities on the river, but campers will find several options available by continuing on to Green River Lake. The last 19 miles of this run, all below Neatsville, are on Green River Lake.

GAUGE: Bridges cross the upper Green at Neatsville, on KY 1640, and at Liberty, thus availing a visual check the water. Green River Lake can be paddled year-round.

GREEN RIVER LAKE DAM TO MUNFORDVILLE

class	I+
gauge	Web, phone
level	Min. 220
	Max. flood (cfs)
velocity	2.6–5.0 (mph)
gradient	1.0 (fpm)
scenery	B

DESCRIPTION: This is a popular canoeing section, and several trip combinations are available. Flow in this section depends on releases from the Green River Lake Dam (the U.S. Army Corps of Engineers has provided adequate water during warm weather months for canoeing). More exposed rock is visible in this section, surrounding terrain is a bit more rugged, and the river is more secluded than in the previous section. Watch for a tall fall entering river right. Averaging 60 feet in width below the dam, the river widens perceptibly to 100–110 feet by the time it reaches Munfordville. Riffles and small rapids enliven the paddling but do not exceed Class I+. Access is good. Deadfalls and an occasional brush jam are the only navigational hazards at normal water levels. Access points in Roachville, Greensburg, the KY 88 bridge, and the US 31E bridge allow for varied trips. Canoe rentals and shuttle service operate on this stretch of the Green.

GAUGE: The USGS Gauge is Green River at Munfordville. The minimum reading should be 220 cfs. In addition, the water release information for Green River Lake Dam can be obtained by calling (270) 465-8824.

Green River
Green River Lake Dam to Munfordville

Points	River Miles	Shuttle Miles
F—G	11.88	14.25
G—H	14.78	8.58
H—I	9.77	13.2
I—J	11.35	7.92
J—K	18.2	19.73
K—L	16.76	9.24
L—M	11.88	11.22

MUNFORDVILLE TO HOUCHINS FERRY

class	I+
gauge	Web
level	Min. 280 Max. flood (cfs)
velocity	0–5.0 (mph)
gradient	1.0 (fpm)
scenery	B

DESCRIPTION: This section of the Green River is also extremely popular, and it runs in large part through the Mammoth Cave National Park. Scenery remains essentially the same as for the river section just described, except that beautiful forests supplant the cornfields once the Green River enters the park, and less exposed rock is evident. Wildlife is abundant in this area, with great variety visible to careful observers. Channeled by the steep surrounding hills, the river averages 70–100 feet wide until it reaches Mammoth Ferry, where it broadens to 130 feet as it encounters the backwater pool of the Brownsville Dam. This point also marks the end of any current or riffles for this section. Needless to say, the Green River here runs through cave country, and at least two caves can be scouted at water's edge. A small cave located a half-mile downstream of Dennison's Ferry on the left bank can actually be paddled into for approximately 40 feet.

Further downstream, about a mile beyond Mammoth Ferry and 200 feet off the river to the left, is a small cave with a beautiful, clear pool of icy water. Canoe camping is allowed throughout the park, but a backcountry fire and camping permit must be obtained from the park rangers (at no charge). Access to the river is good. Deadfalls are the only navigational hazards. This section is runnable all year when the dam is releasing. Shorter runs can be made from Dennisons Ferry and Mammoth Ferry, access points within Mammoth Cave National Park. Outfitters also operate along this stretch of river. It is 21 miles from Munfordville to Dennisons Ferry access on the east side of Mammoth Cave National Park and 7 miles from Dennisons Ferry to Mammoth Ferry. It is 12 miles from Mammoth Ferry to Houchins Ferry.

GAUGE: The USGS Gauge is Green River at Munfordville, also the water release information for Green River Lake Dam can be obtained by calling (270) 465-8824. Also, Mammoth Cave National Park operates a water information line, (270) 758-2166. They note whether the water level at Green River is above 10 feet, at which level the park discourages the launching of self-propelled watercraft.

Green River
Munfordville to Houchins Ferry

bridge
Munfordville

M

31W

65

31W

Horse Cave

65

728

N

Northtown

Dennison's
Ferry

N

**Hart
Co.**

Mammoth
Cave

Deer Park
Hollow Rd.

1827

O

728 1352

Mammoth
Ferry

Maple Springs
Ranger Sta. Rd.

Hart Co.
Edmonson Co.

**MAMMOTH CAVE
NATIONAL
PARK**

**Edmonson
Co.**

Houchins
Ferry Rd.

70

P Houchins
Ferry

To
I-65

101

Brownsville
Dam

70

Q 183

Brownsville

Points	River Miles	Shuttle Miles
M—N	21.12	13.99
N—O	6.5	8.0
O—P	12.0	12.5
P—Q	5.2	4.1

RUSSELL CREEK

Overshadowed by a plethora of nearby paddling destinations, Russell Creek offers solitude and good scenery. From its origins in eastern Adair County, Russell Creek flows northwest, gaining enough tributaries to become floatable at Milltown. From here the Russell meanders north to reach the Green River.

MAPS: Exie, Gresham (USGS)

MILLTOWN TO RUSSELL CREEK ROAD

class	I+
gauge	Web
level	Min. 175 Max. N/A (cfs)
velocity	0.5–3.5 (mph)
gradient	5 (fpm)
scenery	B

DESCRIPTION: Russell Creek is generally runnable from late fall to midsummer and following heavy rains. Fishing is reputed to be good. The Class I waters, generally 30–40 feet wide and bordered by both mud and rock banks, offer enough riffles to keep you moving between pools, finally spilling into the Green River southwest of Greensburg.

Occasional limestone bluffs rise from heavily wooded banks with sycamores aplenty. These thick woods obscure rolling farmlands that lie beyond a paddler's view. Watch for downed trees around tight bends. This section crosses bridges twice between its beginning and end.

GAUGE: The USGS gauge is Russell Creek near Columbia. The minimum reading should be 175 cfs.

RUSSELL CREEK ROAD TO KY 68

class	I+
gauge	Web
level	Min. 200 Max. N/A (cfs)
velocity	0.5–3 (mph)
gradient	1.2 (fpm)
scenery	B

DESCRIPTION: More feeder branches widen the creek a bit and open the canopy in places. Pools are more common than above Russell Creek Road. KY 487 is an alternative put-in for a shorter run. The Green River is located just downstream of the KY 68 take-out. Runs can be extended onto the Green.

GAUGE: The USGS gauge is Russell Creek near Columbia. The minimum reading should be 175 cfs.

BARREN RIVER

The Barren River is one of Kentucky's big rivers. Originating in southern Monroe and Allen Counties near the Tennessee border southeast of Bowling Green, it makes up the main drainage system for a large, four-county area and finally empties into the Green River southeast of Morgantown. It could be very effectively argued that Kentucky's longest and largest river should indeed be the Barren and not the Green. At their confluence, the Barren is easily the larger of the two rivers. Below Barren River Dam the river can be run all year, with easy access at several points. Deadfalls and occasional sandbars at low water are the only hazards to navigation.

MAPS: Lucas, Meador, Parkville, Bowling Green South, Bowling Green North, Hadley, Riverside (USGS)

BARREN RIVER LAKE DAM TO BOWLING GREEN

class	I (II)
gauge	Phone
level	Min. 170 Max. flood (cfs)
velocity	0–2.5 (2.6–5.0) (mph)
gradient	1.3 (fpm)
scenery	B

DESCRIPTION: Runnable year-round from the dam, the Barren River is especially nice and averages 40–60 feet in width upstream from the mouth of Drakes Creek. Along banks of varying steepness, tree roots are exposed by lateral erosion, and the river is more winding. Islands suitable for canoe camping at medium to low water levels are not uncommon. Vegetation is often lush and many hardwoods are in evidence. Occasionally the banks rise steeply with some exposed rock. Between the mouth of Drakes Creek and Jennings Creek, the Barren River is still wide but a little more scenic and interesting for paddling. Running over sand, rock, and clay banks through a deep bed, the river averages from 90 to 150 feet in width. Watch for a Class II man-made rapid on the loop of the river passing through downtown Bowling Green. Other accesses are at G. H. Freemand Park, off Old Louisville Road in Bowling Green, the KY 101 bridge, where KY 234 crosses Bays Fork (put-in only) and Drakes Creek on KY 234 (put-in only). A good but long day trip from the dam to the KY 101 bridge extends 15 miles

ABOUT THE SHUTTLE: To reach the take-out on the west side of Bowling Green from Exit 26 on I-65, take KY 234 West in Bowling Green to KY 185. Turn right on KY 185 and follow it to Boat Landing Road. Turn left on Boat Landing Road to reach James R. Hines Boat Landing Park.

GAUGE: Call the Army Corps of Engineers' Barren River Lake Dam information hotline at (270) 646-2122. It will tell you the water release from below the dam in cubic feet per second. The minimum reading should be 170 cfs.

Barren River
Barren River Lake to Bowling Green

Points	River Miles	Shuttle Miles
A—B	14.59	8.58
B—C	5.72	8.84
C—D	7.29	4.15
D—E	16.87	10.58
E—F	5.71	10.01
F—G	5.15	7.01

BOWLING GREEN TO GREEN RIVER

class	I
gauge	Phone
level	Min. 400 Max. flood (cfs)
velocity	0–2.5 (mph)
gradient	0.7 (fpm)
scenery	C

DESCRIPTION: Downstream from the mouth of Jennings Creek on the west side of Bowling Green, the Barren is a huge river, definitely navigable but not particularly appealing for canoeists. The river is runnable year-round. Access between Bowling Green and the Green River is limited to the area around abandoned Lock 1 by Greencastle near Jenkins Road and near Sallys Rock at the intersection of KY 626 and KY 1435. Lock 1 is a hazard to navigation. Portage is strongly recommended!

ABOUT THE SHUTTLE: To reach the landing just below the confluence of the Barren and Green Rivers, take KY 231 North from Bowling Green toward Morgantown to KY 403. Turn right on KY 403 to reach the landing on the Green River in Woodbury. To reach the put-in on the west side of Bowling Green from Exit 26 on I-65, take KY 234 West in Bowling Green to KY 185. Turn right on KY 185 and follow it to Boat Landing Road. Turn left on Boat Landing Road to reach James R. Hines Boat Landing Park.

GAUGE: Call the Army Corps of Engineers' Barren River Lake Dam information hotline at (270) 646-2122. It will tell you the water release from below the dam in cubic feet per second. Be warned that the river is runnable year-round at this point no matter the release schedule.

Barren River
Bowling Green to Green River

Points	River Miles	Shuttle Miles
G—H	4.43	3.58
H—I	17.16	9.15
I—J	7.44	20.02
J—K	7.72	10.01

DRAKES CREEK

Drakes Creek, along with its three feeder forks, comprises the drainage system for the area directly south of Bowling Green between US 31W on the west and US 231 on the east. Originating near the Tennessee border in Simpson and Allen Counties, Drakes Creek finally empties into the Barren River just outside Bowling Green. Running through deep, rolling farmland and wooded terrain, nearly the entire system provides excellent paddling opportunities. The West Fork and the Trammel Fork are suitable for canoeing, as is Drakes Creek itself below the confluence of the forks. The width of the stream varies from 30 to 45 feet on the forks to 90 feet below the confluence. Deadfalls are not uncommon on the forks but usually do not block the entire stream. Access is excellent with an unusually high number of paved county roads interlacing the entire area.

MAPS: Drake, Allen Springs, Polkville, Bowling Green South (USGS)

CONFLUENCE TO KY 234

class	I+
gauge	Web
level	Min. 120
	Max. flood
	(cfs)
velocity	2.6–5.0
	(mph)
gradient	2.4 (fpm)
scenery	B

DESCRIPTION: The put-in, Romanza Johnson Country Park, is just a bit above the confluence of West Fork and Trammel Fork on Trammel Fork. Drakes Creek below the confluence is runnable most of the year, although an occasional sandbar may have to be portaged during late summer and early fall. Islands, some of which are suitable for canoe camping, can be found below the confluence. The width of the stream widens to 90 feet below the confluence. Shorter trips can be made using the US 231 bridge, the KY 1288 bridge, and Middle Bridge Road bridge. Be careful at the KY 234 bridge because traffic on this road has increased considerably over the past few years.

GAUGE: The USGS gauge is West Fork Drakes Creek near Franklin, KY. The minimum reading should be 120 cfs.

UPPER TRAMMEL FORK TO ROMANZA JOHNSON COUNTRY PARK

class	I+
gauge	Web
level	Min. 150 Max. flood (cfs)
velocity	2.6–5.0 (mph)
gradient	2.4 (fpm)
scenery	B

DESCRIPTION: Running over a sand, rock, and clay bottom, the Trammel Fork of Drakes Creek follows a deep bed overhung by various hardwoods. Watch for low trees and strainers at higher water levels. Boyce-Fairview Road offers an alternate access for a 2-mile trip from KY 240 or a 7-mile trip down to the confluence.

GAUGE: The USGS gauge is West Fork Drakes Creek near Franklin. The minimum reading should be 150 cfs.

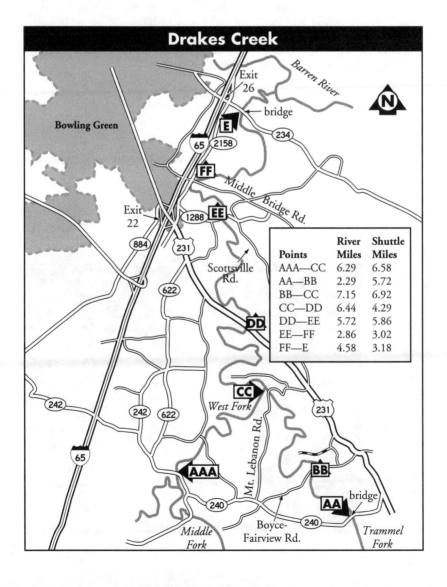

Drakes Creek

Points	River Miles	Shuttle Miles
AAA—CC	6.29	6.58
AA—BB	2.29	5.72
BB—CC	7.15	6.92
CC—DD	6.44	4.29
DD—EE	5.72	5.86
EE—FF	2.86	3.02
FF—E	4.58	3.18

WEST FORK TO
US 231 BRIDGE

class	I+
gauge	Web
level	Min. 150 Max. flood (cfs)
velocity	2.6–5.0 (mph)
gradient	2.4 (fpm)
scenery	B

DESCRIPTION: Banks vary in steepness and sometimes approach the appearance of a gorge on the West Fork where there are some vertical rock walls. Just enough riffles and current are found to make the paddling interesting. The West Fork averages 30–45 feet in width. Pools intersperse very simple (Class I+) shoals and rapids. The water quality is good, and very little trash is found near the stream. The trip could be shortened to 7 miles by pulling upstream at the confluence with Trammel Fork to Romanza Johnson Country Park, which is on Trammel Fork.

GAUGE: The USGS gauge is West Fork Drakes Creek near Franklin. The minimum reading should be 150 cfs.

GASPER RIVER

The Gasper River is one of western Kentucky's most beautiful rivers. It is a tributary of the Barren River and drains the area between Russell- lville and Bowling Green. Runnable from mid-November to mid- May, the Gasper flows over a rock, sand, and clay bottom around medium-sized boulders through a small gorge with steep, exposed rock walls rising almost vertically from the river's edge.

MAPS: South Union, Sugar Grove, Hadley (USGS)

Points	River Miles	Shuttle Miles
A—B	4.58	4.29
B—C	2.29	1.57
C—D	8.72	8.29
D—E	4.86	5.72
E—F	3.58	2.86
F—G	10.73	3.43

BUCKSVILLE TO BARREN RIVER

class	I–II
gauge	Visual
level	Min. 210 Max. 500/flood (cfs)
velocity	2.6–5.0 (mph)
gradient	4.8 (fpm)
scenery	B

DESCRIPTION: The Gasper can be paddled from the Bucksville Road bridge to its mouth at the Barren River. Rated Class II, the Gasper sports a few interesting small rapids and a fairly swift current. Most of the river is very compact, with its width not exceeding 40 feet until just upstream of the KY 626 bridge where the stream broadens to 60–80 feet, though Clear Fork Creek adds significant volume just above the KY 1083 bridge. The upper, narrower sections (above KY 626) are potentially dangerous at high water levels due to frequent strainers (deadfalls) and the lack of eddies. Access from intersecting bridges is not always easy, but it is possible, making runs from 3 to 11 miles possible.

ABOUT THE SHUTTLE: To reach the lowest access point from Exit 7 on the William Natcher Parkway just west of Bowling Green, take US 231 North to KY 626. Turn right on KY 636 to reach KY 1435. Turn right on KY 1435 and pass over the Gasper River bridge; the take-out will be on the left, just upstream on the Barren River. To reach the uppermost access point from Bowling Green, take US 68 South to KY 1083. Turn right on KY 1083 West to reach KY 1038. Turn left on KY 1038 and follow it to Liberty Church Road. Turn left on Liberty Church Road to the Gasper River bridge.

GAUGE: The Gasper is generally high enough to be run from mid-November to mid-May and when the nearby Barren is high and muddy.

LITTLE BARREN RIVER

The Little Barren River, with its east and south forks, drains most of Metcalfe County and the western portion of Green County before emptying into the Green River west of Greensburg. In the upper sections, both forks are runnable. Both of the forks are intimate and scenic, running between steep hills over rock and mud bottoms. Both forks average 30 to 40 feet in width. The river opens up somewhat below the forks. Access is good, and navigational hazards are limited to deadfalls. Access below the confluence of the forks is fair to good (so rated because of a rather difficult access point at the KY 88 bridge). Deadfalls are the primary hazards to navigation.

MAPS: Sulphur Well, East Fork, Center (USGS)

SOUTH FORK LITTLE BARREN RIVER, BEECHVILLE ROAD TO SULPHUR WELL

class	I
gauge	Visual
level	Min. 125
	Max. flood
	(cfs)
velocity	2.6–5.0
	(mph)
gradient	5.7 (fpm)
scenery	B

DESCRIPTION: The South Fork is partially spring-fed and can be run from late October through June downstream of the Beechville Road Ford. A shorter run can be made by starting at the park in the hamlet of Sulphur Well. This section drains more farm country is more prone to staining after heavy rains.

GAUGE: The first few riffles near Beechville Road should give you an idea whether it is floatable. If the South Fork is too low, try the Little Barren from the forks confluence.

EAST FORK LITTLE BARREN RIVER, MELL-CORK ROAD TO KY 745 BRIDGE

class	I+
gauge	Visual
level	Min. 220
	Max. flood
	(cfs)
velocity	2.6–5.0
	(mph)
gradient	9 (fpm)
scenery	B

DESCRIPTION: The East Fork a more interesting run than the South Fork, with small rapids and ledges occurring frequently. The level of difficulty is Class I+. On average, the East Fork can be run from late fall through the spring below the Mell-Cork Road bridge.

GAUGE: The water at the Mell-Cork bridge is a good indicator. If you can run this part, then you should make it all the way down.

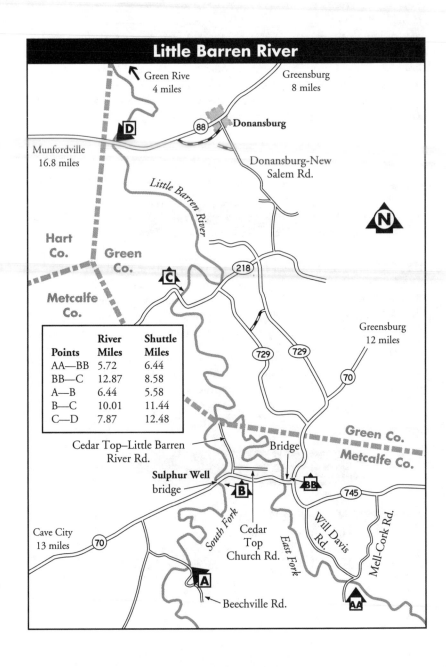

Little Barren River

Green Rive
4 miles

Greensburg
8 miles

Munfordville
16.8 miles

Donansburg

Donansburg-New
Salem Rd.

Little Barren River

Hart
Co.

Green
Co.

Metcalfe
Co.

Greensburg
12 miles

Points	River Miles	Shuttle Miles
AA—BB	5.72	6.44
BB—C	12.87	8.58
A—B	6.44	5.58
B—C	10.01	11.44
C—D	7.87	12.48

Cedar Top–Little Barren
River Rd.

Green Co.

Metcalfe Co.

Bridge

Sulphur Well
bridge

Cave City
13 miles

South Fork

Cedar
Top
Church Rd.

East Fork

Will Davis Rd.

Mell-Cork Rd.

Beechville Rd.

Little Barren River, Confluence of East Fork and South Fork to KY 88

class	1+
gauge	Visual
level	Min. 220 Max. flood (cfs)
velocity	2.6–5.0 (mph)
gradient	3.3 (fpm)
scenery	B

DESCRIPTION: The valley deepens below the confluence of the two forks, with more exposed rock visible. The river widens to an average of 50–60 feet. Banks are 20 feet high here and generally steep. As the Little Barren approaches its mouth at the Green River, sandbars become more numerous, and the steeper terrain of southern Green and northern Metcalfe Counties gives way to more gently rolling farm- and woodland. A shorter run can be made using KY 218 as an access.

ABOUT THE SHUTTLE: From Greensburg, take KY 81 to KY 88. Turn left on KY 88 and follow it past the Green River to the Little Barren River. To reach the put-in, take KY 70 to Cedar Top Church Road (make sure and pick up Cedar Top Church Road west of where KY 70 and US 68 diverge). Turn right on Cedar Top Church Road, then quickly take a left on Cedar Top-Little Barren River Road to the confluence of the East Fork and South Fork.

GAUGE: There is no gauge. However, of the runs in the Little Barren River watershed, this section can be floated year-round, except for periods of extreme dryness.

NOLIN RIVER

The Nolin River winds out of the hilly farm country of Hardin County and flows south along the Grayson–Hart County line to empty into Nolin River Lake. Below the Nolin Dam in Edmonson County, the Nolin continues south to its confluence with the Green River in Mammoth Cave National Park. Because the stream is bordered without exception by private property, canoe camping is only recommended within the confines of Nolin River Lake and below the Nolin River Lake Dam within Mammoth Cave National Park. The level of difficulty is Class I, although small shoals and riffles and a good current keep the paddling from becoming tedious.

MAPS: Sonora, Summit, Millerstown, Cub Run, Nolin Reservoir, Rhoda (USGS), Mammoth Cave National Park map

STAR MILLS TO NOLIN RIVER LAKE

class	I
gauge	Visual
level	Min. 250
	Max. flood (cfs)
velocity	0–5.0 (mph)
gradient	2.1 (fpm)
scenery	B

DESCRIPTION: An attractive, tree-lined river averaging 35–50 feet wide, the Nolin flows between steep banks over a rock and mud bottom. Throughout the upper sections in Hardin County, the terrain is gently rolling with farms adjoining the river. South of Star Mills, the river valley deepens, with steep hills rising from time to time along the west bank. From this point to the headwaters of Nolin River Lake, the stream is interrupted four times by the remnants of dams from a once-flourishing mill industry. Although signs of human habitation are common, regal hardwoods (mostly old growth) overhanging the stream help keep the beauty and the tranquil atmosphere of the stream intact. The Nolin River is runnable from late fall to midsummer from KY 84 to Wheelers Mill. From Wheelers Mill to the headwaters of the lake, the Nolin is runnable all year long. Access for all varied runs above the lake is good, except on KY 1375 at Star Mills, where access is possible but difficult. Dangers in these upper sections include deadfalls, and, as mentioned, dams. All of the dams can be portaged without difficulty except at extremely high water levels. With the exception of the dam at Star Mills, all of the dams are extremely dangerous and should not be run for any reason. At Star Mills, however, the dam has collapsed in two places, creating artificial Class II+ (borderline Class III) rapids. These rapids are runnable but should be scouted anew at every different water level. The last 24 miles of this section are on Nolin River Lake. It is 11 miles from KY 1868 to White Mills, 8 more miles to Spurrier, and 14 miles from Spurrier to the KY 1214 bridge.

GAUGE: This is a look-and-see proposition. The upper Nolin is generally runnable from November to late June.

Nolin River
KY 1868 to Nolin River Lake

Points	River Miles	Shuttle Miles
A—B	4.5	5.0
B—C	6.5	5.0
C—D	2.0	1.5
D—E	6.0	6.0
E—F	4.0	2.5
F—G	10.5	8.0
G—H	28.6	24.31
H—I	1.43	17.16

NOLIN RIVER DAM TO HOUCHINS FERRY ON GREEN RIVER

class	I
length	9
time	5
gauge	Web
level	250
gradient	2.2
scenery	B+

DESCRIPTION: From the tailwaters of the Nolin River Dam to the mouth of the Nolin at the Green River, the stream flows through the backcountry woodlands of Mammoth Cave National Park. This section of the Nolin is especially scenic with high, exposed bluffs and plentiful wildlife, particularly deer and ducks. This section is only 9 miles long (including an easy 2-mile paddle upstream on the Green to the take-out at Houchins Ferry) but affords some beautiful camping spots for those with a short way to go and a long time to get there. A Mammoth Cave National Park, backcountry camping permit is required. Once again, the level of difficulty is Class I but with a good current. The lower section of the Nolin River is usually runnable all year but is entirely dependent on releases at the dam for adequate flow. Navigational hazards are limited to deadfalls. The average stream width is 50–80 feet. Access is good.

GAUGE: The Nolin below the dam is runnable year-round. However, check the Army Corps of Engineers Nolin River Lake Web site, http://www.lrl.usace.army.mil/wc/reports/lkreport.html, to see the 6 a.m. outflow and get the cfs release from the dam. The minimum should be 250 cfs.

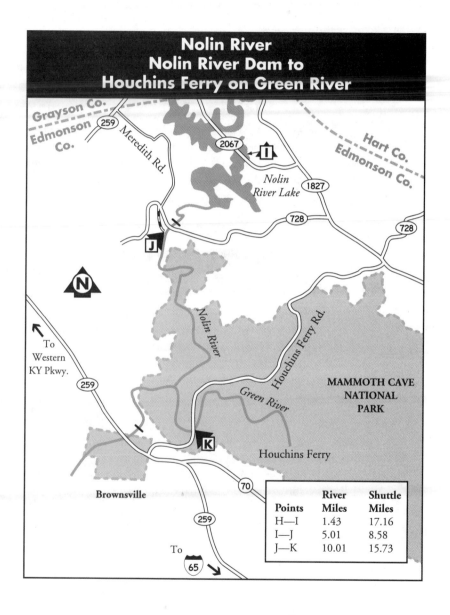

Nolin River
Nolin River Dam to
Houchins Ferry on Green River

Grayson Co.
Edmonson Co.

259

Meredith Rd.

2067

I

Nolin River Lake

1827

728

728

J

N

To Western KY Pkwy.

259

Nolin River

Houchins Ferry Rd.

Green River

MAMMOTH CAVE NATIONAL PARK

K

Houchins Ferry

Brownsville

70

259

To

65

Hart Co.
Edmonson Co.

Points	River Miles	Shuttle Miles
H—I	1.43	17.16
I—J	5.01	8.58
J—K	10.01	15.73

TRADEWATER RIVER

Everyone in western Kentucky knows about the tragedy of the Tradewater River—that sterile, lifeless stream appropriated as a private sewer for the mining industry. The Tradewater River runs north from Christian County and empties into the Ohio River west of Sturgis.

MAPS: Dawson Springs, Olney, Dalton, Providence, Blackford, Sturgis, Dekoven (USGS)

KY 70 TO OHIO RIVER

class	I
gauge	Web
level	Min. 130 Max. flood (cfs)
velocity	0–2.5 (mph)
gradient	0.7 (fpm)
scenery	C–

DESCRIPTION: Although the water is almost devoid of life, the stream is nevertheless pleasing to the eye. An intimate river, with willow and hardwood completely shading the water, it winds through rolling farm and mining country. The river channel is generally deep, thereby facilitating paddling, and it is not normally cluttered with deadfalls downstream of the KY 120 bridge. The Tradewater River is generally runnable most of the year downstream of the KY 293 bridge, although an occasional shallow may have to be portaged in late summer and early fall. However, the river is more appealing further upstream. The bottom and banks of the river are mud and vary markedly in their degree of slope. Cypress trees are abundant. The gradient is gentle, and current is moderate to slow. The river expands from 35 feet in width at the KY 293 bridge to around 110 feet near its mouth.

Numerous access points allow for trips of varied lengths. Canoe camping near the stream is possible at low water levels. Access at bridge intersections is fair to good.

GAUGE: The USGS Gauge is Tradewater River at Olney. The minimum reading should be 130 cfs.

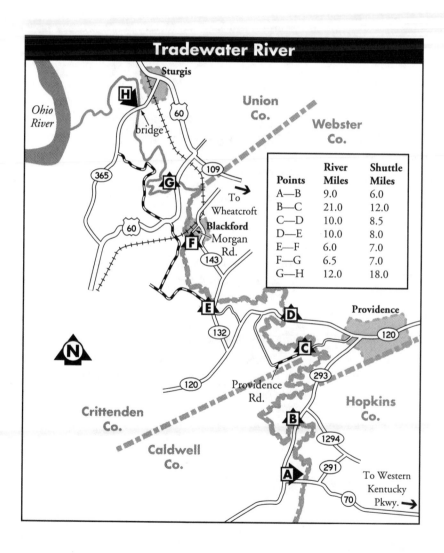

Tradewater River

Points	River Miles	Shuttle Miles
A—B	9.0	6.0
B—C	21.0	12.0
C—D	10.0	8.5
D—E	10.0	8.0
E—F	6.0	7.0
F—G	6.5	7.0
G—H	12.0	18.0

POND RIVER

The Pond River is a main tributary of the Green River. Its headwaters are in northern Todd County, and its mouth is west of Calhoun on the McLean–Hopkins border. The Pond River and its tributaries, all of which are small, are the main drainage system for eastern Hopkins, western Muhlenberg, northern Christian, and northern Todd Counties. Although the water quality is not the best due to some mining discharge, the stream is nevertheless scenic, with birch and willow trees overhanging the water, and it has a well-defined, navigable channel.

MAPS: Millport, Sacramento, Calhoun (USGS)

KY 70 TO GREEN RIVER

class	I
gauge	Web
level	Min. 170 Max. flood (cfs)
velocity	0–2.5 (2.6–5.0) (mph)
gradient	0.8 (fpm)
scenery	C

DESCRIPTION: The Pond River is generally runnable all year from the KY 70 bridge to its mouth, although occasional shallows may have to be portaged in late summer and early fall. The river is generally clear of deadfalls and debris, but some may be encountered upstream of KY 85 bridge, particularly after spring flooding. At the intersection of KY 70, the Pond River is about 25 feet wide. Moving north, it stays small (under 50 feet) up to within 10 miles of its mouth where it broadens to 80–100 feet. The river flows through gently rolling, flat farmland and occasionally through some woodland and mining country. Its bottom is of mud with generally high, steep banks. Access is fair to good at most bridge crossings. Current is slow (less than 2 mph), except at high water. Riverside areas for canoe camping are limited (even at low water) by the steep banks and the dense streamside vegetation. It is possible, however, to secure permission (in advance) to camp on the edge of the farm fields above the river if you contact the landowners in person.

GAUGE: The USGS gauge is Pond River near Apex. The minimum reading should be 170 cfs.

Pond River

Webster Co.

McLean Co.

Green River

Calhoun

81

Ashbyburg

370

138

138

Jewel City   bridge   **D**

Hensel Martin Rd.

Bell Rd.

← To Exit 54

Hopkins Co.

Branch Schoolhouse Rd.

1155

81

C

254

254

Sacremento

Points	River Miles	Shuttle Miles
A—B	9.0	10.5
B—C	5.5	7.0
C—D	6.0	11.0

McLean Co.

B

81

85

Muhlenberg Co.

To Exit 42

Hopkins Co.

N

70/85   70   **A**

PANTHER CREEK

Panther Creek constitutes the main drainage system for Daviess County and the area around Owensboro. The creek is canoeable but definitely not aesthetically pleasing.

MAPS: Sutherland, Panther, Curdsville (USGS)

KY 81 TO GREEN RIVER

class	I
gauge	Visual
level	Min. 95
	Max. flood
	(cfs)
velocity	0–2.5 (mph)
gradient	0.6 (fpm)
scenery	D

DESCRIPTION: Panther Creek is narrow, resembles a dredged drainage ditch, and has been denuded of all but scrub vegetation 15 feet from its banks, presumably for the purpose of terracing. The Panther runs through flat farmland. Its banks and bottom are of mud, steep, and 6–15 feet high. Water quality is poor. Access from intersecting bridges is usually not difficult.

GAUGE: The creek is generally runnable from late fall through late spring.

Panther Creek

Ohio River

60

Owensboro

BYP 60

Panther Cr.

N

431

431

554

Exit 2

81

Wayne Br. Rd.

A

81

bridge

60

279

279

279

Audubon Pkwy.

56

Hayden Br. Rd.

815

456

56

To Henderson 19.4 miles

bridge

500

B

Green River

Points	River Miles	Shuttle Miles
A—B	21.74	17.16

ROUGH RIVER

The Rough River is not very rough but extremely canoeable. Running east to west over a rock bottom through wooded hill country and farmland, the Rough River is typically high-banked and shaded with willow and various hardwoods. The Rough can be paddled all year from the tailwater of the Rough River Lake Dam to its mouth at the Green River near Livermore. Water quality is generally fair to good. Lateral erosion along the steep banks has exposed many tree roots and has caused a substantial number of deadfalls. The river's width averages from 50 to 70 feet throughout.

MAPS: McDaniels, Falls of Rough, Olaton, Dundee, Horton, Equality (USGS)

ROUGH RIVER DAM TO DUNDEE

class	I (II)
gauge	Web
level	Min. 165
	Max. flood (cfs)
velocity	0–5.0 (mph)
gradient	1.4 (fpm)
scenery	B

DESCRIPTION: The most scenic sections are from the tailwater to Falls of the Rough, and from Falls of the Rough to the KY 54 bridge. Both of these sections sport some minor (Class I+) rapids, ripples, and shoals and occasional bluffs. The take-out at the KY 110 bridge requires a major uphill pull. The land around the 7-foot dam at Falls of the Rough and old stores and buildings of the Falls of Rough community are now part of a golf course and resort. Ask for permission at the resort entrance station before portaging around the dam at Falls of Rough or using the area as a put-in or take-out. The dam itself is considered extremely dangerous and should not be run under any circumstances. Several access points allow trips of varied lengths. It is 5 miles from the dam to Falls of Rough, 8 miles from Falls of Rough to Hite Falls, and 10 miles farther to Dundee.

GAUGE: The Rough below the dam is runnable year-round. Check the Army Corps of Engineers Rough River Lake Web site, http://www.lrl.usace.army.mil/wc/reports/lkreport.html, to see the 6 a.m. outflow to get an idea of the cfs release from the dam.

Rough River
Rough River Dam to Dundee

Rough River Lake

79

54

Tailwater
Recreation Area

A

110

N

B

*Falls of
the Rough*

Hite
Falls

110

54

C

Breckinridge
Co.

Grayson
Co.

Ohio
Co.

Shreve
Rd.

Ohio
Co.

919

54

878

Narrows

D

Fordsville

E

919

69

F

Dundee

bridge

69

Points	River Miles	Shuttle Miles
A—B	5.0	4.0
B—C	8.0	12.0
C—D	11.0	14.2
D—E	2.5	1.8
E—F	2.0	2.0

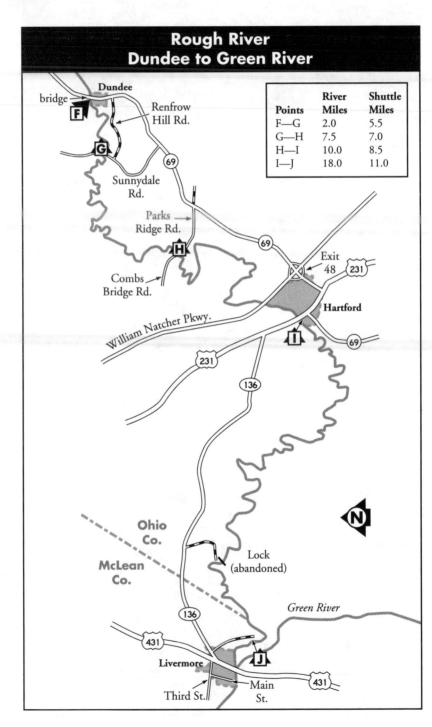

Rough River
Dundee to Green River

Points	River Miles	Shuttle Miles
F—G	2.0	5.5
G—H	7.5	7.0
H—I	10.0	8.5
I—J	18.0	11.0

bridge

Dundee

F

Renfrow Hill Rd.

G

69

Sunnydale Rd.

Parks Ridge Rd.

H

69

Exit 48

231

Combs Bridge Rd.

William Natcher Pkwy.

Hartford

I

69

231

136

N

Ohio Co.

McLean Co.

Lock (abandoned)

Green River

136

431

Livermore

J

Third St.

Main St.

431

DUNDEE TO GREEN RIVER

class	I
gauge	Web
level	Min. 190 Max. flood (cfs)
velocity	0–5.0 (mph)
gradient	0.6 (fpm)
scenery	C+

DESCRIPTION: Moving further downstream, access is limited downstream from the public boat ramp just west of Hartford, requiring an 18-mile run from Hartford to Livermore. Shorter floats are much easier near Dundee, including a 7.5-mile trip from Sunnydale Road to Combs Bridge Road. From Hartford to the mouth of the Rough near Livermore, silver maples line the watercourse. Watch out for and portage around the abandoned U.S. Army Corps of Engineers lock a few miles upstream of Livermore.

ABOUT THE SHUTTLE: To reach the take-out in Livermore from Exit 48 on William Natcher Parkway, take KY 69 to Hartford. Turn right and head north on US 231 to KY 136. Turn left on KY 136 and follow it to US 431. Turn left and take US 431 South to Third Street. Turn right on Third Street, then turn left on Main Street, which leads to a boat ramp on the Green River just below the confluence with the Rough River. To reach the put-in from Exit 48 on Natcher Parkway, take KY 69 North to Dundee and bridge over Rough River.

GAUGE: The Rough below the dam is runnable year-round. However, check the Army Corps of Engineers Rough River Lake Web site, http://www.lrl.usace.army.mil/wc/reports/lkreport.html, to see the 6 a.m. outflow to get an idea of the cfs release from the dam.

MUD RIVER

The Mud River is an uninspiring stream originating near Russellville and running north over a mud bottom to empty into the Green River at Rochester. It is runnable from late fall to midsummer from the KY 949 bridge to its mouth.

MAPS: Dunmor, Rochester (USGS)

KY 949 TO ROCHESTER

class	I
gauge	Visual
level	Min. 120
	Max. flood (cfs)
velocity	0–2.5 (mph)
gradient	0.6 (fpm)
scenery	D

DESCRIPTION: Access is good at bridge crossings and at the mouth but almost totally lacking in between. The Mud River runs primarily through hilly farmland. Banks are well vegetated and tree-lined, but the water quality is poor due to mining waste discharge. Its width varies markedly from about 35 feet at the KY 949 bridge to almost 100 feet upstream of the KY 70 bridge. Deadfalls and some trash are in evidence on the narrower upstream sections.

SHUTTLE: To reach the lower access from Exit 28 on William Natcher Parkway, take KY 70 West to KY 2263. Turn right on

KY 2263, then immediately turn left into the Rochester boat ramp, on the Green River. To reach the upper access from Exit 28 on William Natcher Parkway, take KY 70 West to KY 106. Turn left on KY 106 to KY 949. Turn right on KY 949 and follow it to bridge over Mud River.

GAUGE: Look to run the Mud from mid-November to early July or when the Green River is high.

Points	River Miles	Shuttle Miles
A—B	15.7	7.5

GREEN RIVER
FROM HOUCHINS FERRY TO THE OHIO RIVER

This long, 185-mile section of the Green River is runnable all year, and access is plentiful, but unfortunately so are powerboats, barges, locks, and dams. In short, the lower Green River is one of Kentucky's primary commercial waterways and is not consistently appealing to paddlers. (Note: The upstream sections of the Green River are found in Part Seven: Headwaters of the Green River.)

MAPS: Rhoda, Brownsville, Reedyville, Riverside, Morgantown, Flener, Cromwell, South Hill, Rochester, Paradise, Central City East, Central City West, Equality, Livermore, Glenville, Calhoun, Beech Grove, Delaware, Curdsville, Reed, Spottsville, Newburgh (USGS)

HOUCHINS FERRY TO ROCHESTER

class	I
gauge	Web
level	Min. 4 ft. Max. flood
velocity	0–2.5 (2.6–5.0) (mph)
gradient	0.5 (fpm)
scenery	C+

DESCRIPTION: From Houchins Ferry the Green River broadens considerably (increasing in volume) at its confluence with the Nolin River. Two miles farther downstream is the Brownsville Dam, a difficult portage at the old Lock 6. Old Lock 5 at Naker and old Lock 4 at Woodbury have been abandoned but nevertheless remain a danger to navigation. Portages are a must! From the dam to the mouth of the Barren River the scenery remains pleasant, with farms and wooded hills. It is 35 miles from Houchins Ferry to Woodbury, 6 miles farther to Morgantown, and 37 miles from Morgantown to Rochester.

GAUGE: The USGS gauge is Green River/Lock 6 at Brownsville. The minimum reading should be 4 feet. This part of the Green is runnable year-round.

Green River
Houchins Ferry to Rochester

Green River

Nolin River

Houchins Ferry

70

183

Lock 6
(dam still here)

Q

Brownsville

Edmonson Co.

N

Davis Ferry Rd.

655

Windyville
Honakers Ferry Rd.

R

1749

T

S

Naker

185

U

Warren Co.

65

Lock 5
(abandoned)

Edmonson Co.

Butler Co.

Green River

Barren River

Bowling Green

231

70

Lock 4
(abandoned)

V

William Natcher Pkwy.

Exit 7

Warren Co.

Butler Co.

403   403

231

Morgantown

W

231

Exit 27
Exit 28

403 269

Z

Y

Mining City

X

1117

70

Beaver Dam
13.7 miles

369

Rochester

AA

Skillsville

Lock 3
(abandoned)

BB

Mud River

Muhlenberg Co.

Points	River Miles	Shuttle Miles
Q—R	11.44	10.1
R—S	2.86	3.58
S—T	0.5	0.7
T—U	2.15	3.0
U—V	18.59	32.18
V—W	6.01	6.44
W—X	14.30	15.02
X—Y	7.15	10.01
Y—Z	5.72	16.45
Z—AA	9.3	8.58
AA—BB	0.86	1.5

ROCHESTER TO MOUTH OF POND RIVER

class	I
gauge	Web
level	Min. 340
	Max. flood
	(cfs)
velocity	0–2.5
	(2.6–5.0)
	(mph)
gradient	0.4 (fpm)
scenery	C+

DESCRIPTION: Old Lock 3 at Rochester, just above the put-in for this section, is abandoned. Put your boat in well below the flow. In this stretch, pleasure boaters constitute the majority of river traffic. As on any big river, the vistas are panoramic (if not often changing), access is excellent by virtue of the many small marinas, and countless trip possibilities exist. It is 26 miles from Rochester to Central City, 17 miles from Central City to Livermore, 10 miles from Livermore to Calhoun, and 10 more miles to the mouth of the Pond River.

Green River
Rochester to Mouth of Pond River

Points	River Miles	Shuttle Miles
AA—BB	0.86	1.5
BB—CC	8.58	13.59
CC—DD	5.72	7.15
DD—EE	10.73	12.87
EE—FF	12.16	15.73
FF—GG	5.01	9.3
GG—HH	10.01	11.44
HH—II	0.72	1.43
II—JJ	9.3	8.58

ABOUT SHUTTLE: To reach the Rochester access from Exit 58 on the Western Kentucky Parkway, take US 431 South to KY 70. Turn left on KY 70 and follow it east to KY 2263 and the bridge over Mud River. Look for a gravel road leading left to Muhlenburg County Park and boat ramp below old Lock 3. The county park and boat ramp are before KY 2263 and the bridge over Mud River. Do not put in at Rochester boat ramp, as this will be above old Lock 3.

GAUGE: The USGS gauge is Green River at Livermore. The minimum reading should be 5 feet. This part of the Green is runnable year-round.

MOUTH OF POND RIVER TO OHIO RIVER

class	I
gauge	Web
level	Min. 6 ft. Max. flood
velocity	2.6–5.0 (mph)
gradient	0.4 (fpm)
scenery	C

DESCRIPTION: The river, runnable year-round down here, belongs to the coal industry. But although coal tipples, rail yards, and barges are frequently in evidence, the lower Green is not totally lacking in charm. Navigational hazards consist almost exclusively of the well-marked locks and dams. Lock 2 and Lock 1 are still in operation. Exercise caution around these facilities. The Spottsville take-out is above Lock 1. It is 19 miles from the mouth of the Pond River to Rangers Landing on KY 136 and 23 miles farther to the Ohio River.

ABOUT THE SHUTTLE: To reach the lowest access from Exit 81 on Breathitt Parkway, take US 60 East to Spottsville. Turn right on Spring Street just before the bridge over Green River and stay left with KY 2243 to turn left on Olhend-Spottsville Road and reach the Joe Pruden Boat Ramp at Willow Creek on the Green River one-half mile above Lock 1. To reach the upper access from Exit 54 on Breathitt Parkway, take KY 138 East to the bridge over the Pond River just above the Green River.

GAUGE: The USGS gauge is Green River at Lock 2/Calhoun. The minimum reading should be 6 feet.

Green River
Mouth of Pond River to Ohio River

Breathitt Pkwy.

Ohio River

Henderson Co.

QQ

Exit 81

Daviess Co.

1078

60

Spottsville 2243

PP

Lock 1

Henderson

60

1078

Spring St.

OO

351

Audubon Pkwy.

416

NN

Curdsville Rd.

416

N

136

Daviess Co.

Henderson Co.

41

MM

Rangers Landing

McLean Co.

Webster Co.

LL

56

136

Eastwood Ferry Rd.

Beech Grove

147

KK

256

1792

Calhoun

Wrightsburg

Onton

Points	River Miles	Shuttle Miles
JJ—KK	9.0	9.5
KK—LL	8.0	6.01
LL—MM	2.2	4.86
MM—NN	7.15	10.01
NN—OO	9.15	13.59
OO—PP	3.00	7.87
PP—QQ	3.15	2.86

370

81

Breathitt Pkwy.

JJ

Webster Co.

138

Hopkins Co.

Pond River

Exit 54

part**Nine**

CUMBERLAND RIVER NORTH OF LAKE BARKLEY

This section of the Cumberland River flows northwest from the tail-waters of Barkley Dam through Livingston County to the Ohio River. Pleasant but decidedly unspectacular, the Cumberland River makes long, graceful curves through the hilly farmland east of Paducah.

MAPS: Grand Rivers, Dycusburg, Burna, Smithland (USGS)

BARKLEY DAM TO OHIO RIVER

class	I
gauge	Phone
level	Min. N/A
	Max. N/A
velocity	0–2.5 (mph)
gradient	0.4 (fpm)
scenery	C+

DESCRIPTION: Trees (primarily willow) line the riverside but do not consistently obstruct the paddler's view of surrounding farms, small towns, and occasional businesses. The average width below the dam is 240 feet Powerboats of all sizes are common. This section of the Cumberland is runnable all year. Access is good. The level of difficulty is Class I, with no navigational dangers except powerboats.

GAUGE: Call the TVA Lake Information Line at (800) 238-2264, then press 4, then 40, to get the latest water release from Barkley Lake Dam in cfs.

Cumberland River North of Lake Barkley
Tennessee River North of Kentucky Lake

Logan Co.

Eddyville
8 Miles

Lake Barkley

641
62

B

70

917

723

C

Livingston Co.

Cumberland River

Exit 31

453

453

Barkley Dam

282

A

Kentucky Lake

641

Exit 27

70

Haddock Ferry Rd.

453

C

Marshall Co.

Tennessee River

62

60

Boat Ramp

Smithland

453

D

24

Ohio River

Marshall Co.

McCracken Co.

60

62

B

Clarks River

Points	River Miles	Shuttle Miles
A—B	9.0	11.0
B—C	3.5	4.0
C—D	12.5	10.0

TENNESSEE RIVER NORTH OF KENTUCKY LAKE

This 16-mile section of the Tennessee River flowing north along the southern boundary of Livingston County is all that is left of the beautiful Tennessee River in the state of Kentucky.

MAPS: Calvert City, Little Cypress, Paducah East (USGS)

KENTUCKY DAM TO MOUTH OF CLARKS RIVER

class	I
gauge	Phone
level	Min. N/A
	Max. N/A
velocity	0–2.5 (mph)
gradient	0.3 (fpm)
scenery	C

DESCRIPTION: Averaging 200–250 feet in width, this section of the Tennessee accommodates almost continuous commercial traffic. Scenery is similar to that of the Cumberland River below Barkley Dam except that the river valley here is somewhat deeper. Runnable all year, access is good where it exists. The level of difficulty is Class I with powercraft, particularly barges, constituting the major danger to paddlers.

ABOUT THE SHUTTLE: To reach the take-out at the mouth of the Clarks River from Exit 16 on I-24, take US 68 West to US 62. Turn left and take US 62 West to Clarks River boat ramp below bridge over Clarks River. To reach the put-in below Kentucky Dam from Exit 27 on I-24, take US 62 East to KY 282. Take KY 282 West to Cirrito Lane. Turn right on Cirrito Lane to reach a boat ramp on the river.

GAUGE: Call the TVA Lake Information Line at (800) 238-2264, then press 4, then 33 to get the water release from Kentucky Lake Dam in cfs.

MUDDY FORK OF THE LITTLE RIVER

The Muddy Fork of the Little River originates in western Christian County and flows west to drain northern Trigg County before emptying into Lake Barkley.

MAPS: Cobb, Cadiz, Lamasco, Canton (USGS)

ADAMS MILL ROAD BRIDGE TO LAKE BARKLEY

class	I+
gauge	Web
level	Min. 220 Max. flood (cfs)
velocity	0–5.0 (mph)
gradient	0.7 (fpm)
scenery	B–

DESCRIPTION: The Muddy Fork (not to be confused with the Mud River) is in many ways an inviting, intimate stream. The banks are steep, profusely shaded with tall hardwoods, and from time to time exposed rock is visible at water's edge. Averaging 35 feet in width, the Muddy Fork can be run from late fall to mid-summer downstream of the Adams Mill bridge, and its proximity to Lake Barkley makes canoe camping possible. Scenery streamside consists of rolling farm- and woodland (which you cannot see except in winter because of the dense foliage along the banks). The level of difficulty is Class I throughout with deadfalls (and some flash flooding in the upper sections) being the only hazards to navigation. Steep banks make access fair to difficult.

GAUGE: The USGS gauge is Little River near Cadiz. The minimum reading should be 220 cfs.

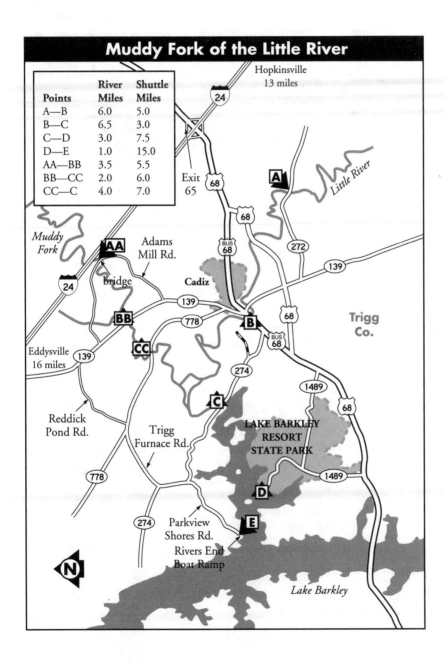

Muddy Fork of the Little River

Points	River Miles	Shuttle Miles
A—B	6.0	5.0
B—C	6.5	3.0
C—D	3.0	7.5
D—E	1.0	15.0
AA—BB	3.5	5.5
BB—CC	2.0	6.0
CC—C	4.0	7.0

Hopkinsville 13 miles

Little River

Muddy Fork

Adams Mill Rd.

bridge

Cadiz

Exit 65

Trigg Co.

Eddysville 16 miles

Reddick Pond Rd.

Trigg Furnace Rd.

LAKE BARKLEY RESORT STATE PARK

Parkview Shores Rd.

Rivers End Boat Ramp

Lake Barkley

N

LITTLE RIVER

The Little River originates in southern Christian County and flows north through Cadiz in Trigg County before emptying into Lake Barkley. The upper section is winding and tree-lined with some giant, virgin timber. Terrain is hilly and rolling. The banks and bed are of mud with thick vegetation near the river's edge.

MAPS: Roaring Spring, Caledonia, Cadiz, Cobb, Lamasco, Canton (USGS)

KY 272 TO LAKE BARKLEY

class	I+
gauge	Web
level	Min. 200
	Max. flood
	(cfs)
velocity	0–5 (mph)
gradient	1.0 (fpm)
scenery	B

DESCRIPTION: A good canoe-camping run, the Little River is runnable below the KY 272 bridge to Cadiz (there is a boat ramp at the US 68 bridge) from November to mid-July and from Cadiz to Lake Barkley all year long. Access is good. Some deadfalls, a fallen bridge, and a small 1-foot dam pose the only difficulties to navigation. From Cadiz downstream there is no current due to the backed-up lake pool. It is 6 miles from KY 272 to the slack pool in Cadiz. The river broadens from 45 feet in the upper stretches to 60–75 feet below Cadiz. Surrounding hillsides are steeper with some exposed rock visible. There are no real hazards to navigation below Cadiz except an occasional gusty wind coming off the lake. Access is excellent, especially the Army Corps of Engineers ramps and Lake Barkley State Park marina. Runs on the Little River can readily be combined with trips of various lengths on Lake Barkley.

ABOUT THE SHUTTLE: To reach the lowest access on Lake Barkley from Exit 65 on I-24, take US 68 West to US 68 Business to KY 274. Turn right on KY 274 and follow it to Parkview Shores Road. Turn left on Parkview Shores Road and follow it to the Rivers End Boat Ramp. To reach the uppermost access from Exit 65 on I-24, take US 68 West to KY 139. Turn left on KY 139 and follow it to KY 272. Turn left and take KY 272 East to bridge over Little River.

GAUGE: The USGS gauge is Little River near Cadiz. The minimum reading should be 200 cfs.

LAND BETWEEN THE LAKES PADDLE ROUTE

Look at a map of the United States, then focus on middle America. Try to find any body of water with 300 miles of undeveloped shoreline. Only one place offers such a shoreline—Land between the Lakes. Here paddlers in both canoes and sea kayaks can travel along the bays and bluffs of Kentucky Lake and Lake Barkley. Adventurous paddlers will circumnavigate the long peninsula of the LBL, making nearly a loop separated by less than 10 miles of land. Paddlers can go for days without backtracking and still end up fairly close to their car and point of origin. The 85 miles is the shortest possible route of an LBL peninsula circumnavigation without exploring bays or making any side trips. A look at the map will show that this route can be extended by many miles and from five days to over two weeks.

This circumnavigation of the LBL peninsula is what I call the Land between the Lakes Paddle Route, the best paddling area in middle America. The route begins on Kentucky Lake at Boswell Landing Lake Access in Tennessee. Paddlers then head north along Kentucky Lake, passing many big bays while heading north into Kentucky. Lake accesses and campgrounds occasionally break wild shoreline. The Kentucky Dam eventually comes into view. Here, paddlers take Barkley Canal, joining Kentucky Lake to Lake Barkley. Paddlers may experience a strong current here. Which way this current flows depends on which watershed—the Tennessee River or the Cumberland River—have received more rainfall recently.

Paddlers leave the canal, heading east, past Kuttawa Landing Lake Access. Beyond here, Lake Barkley turns south, and paddlers pass the largest bays of Barkley. Islands appear more frequently south of the US 68/KY 80 bridge. Finally, paddlers reenter the Volunteer State and end the paddle route at the boat launch near Gatlin Point Campground. From here, it is but 10 miles by road to Boswell Landing.

MAPS: Rushing Creek, Fenton, Fairdealing, Birmingham Point, Grand Rivers, Eddyville, Mont, Canton, Linton (USGS); Land between the Lakes National Recreation Area map

KENTUCKY LAKE: BOSWELL LANDING TO NICKELL BRANCH

class	I
gauge	Visual
level	N/A
velocity	N/A
gradient	N/A
scenery	A

DESCRIPTION: The LBL Paddle Route is broken into two segments, Kentucky Lake and Lake Barkley. This first segment begins at Boswell Landing and travels north for 35 miles along the northernmost end of Kentucky Lake. Add 1 more mile passing through the Barkley Canal, the canal connecting Kentucky Lake and Lake Barkley. Boswell Landing makes for a good starting spot with its courtesy dock and boat ramp. From here, paddlers can see far north up Kentucky Lake. On entering the water, paddlers will be surprised at the width of the river—easily a mile wide. This width can cause problems if a big wind kicks up. However, the biggest surprise may be the changing character of the wild shoreline—hilly, tree-covered banks, rock bluffs, clay bluffs, and gravel bars all melded into a winding border between water and land.

There is so much shoreline to explore—deep bays with numerous arms leading up quiet coves cutting deep into the heart of LBL beg to be paddled. On the main lake, civilization is barely visible across the water. Occasional giant barge loads pushed by humming tugs ply the old bed of the Tennessee River channel. Pleasure boaters and fishing boats will be seen, especially on weekends.

Pine Bluff stands far above the lake 5 miles north of Boswell Landing. Ginger Bay Lake Access lies 2 miles north of the bluff. No services are offered. The gravel bars on the main shoreline are your best bet for camping on Kentucky Lake. The landings are easy. However, if you should choose more developed camping, Rushing Creek Campground, with potable water and hot showers, lies in a small cove on the main shore 10 miles north of Boswell. Enter Kentucky just beyond Rushing Creek. A large shoreline sign marks the boundary. Anglers must have a fishing license for each state in which they are fishing.

Redd Hollow Lake Access lies in a cove 2 miles north of the state line. Kentucky Lake narrows a bit. Beyond here, the Eggners Ferry Bridge becomes visible. Fenton Campground (with potable water) is on the LBL shoreline just before the bridge. Kenlake State Park is on the western shore by the bridge. The lake widens again north of the bridge. Here, deeply cut bays are interspersed along the main shoreline. Exploration opportunities are numerous along this wild shore. The rocky point just south of Higgins Bay makes for a good breaking spot.

Things become more developed far north. Smith Bay, part of Birmingham Ferry campground, 28 miles north of Boswell, marks the beginning of this developed area. Just ahead is large Hillman Ferry Campground, which offers water and hot showers. The north end of the campground is closer to the main lake channel. Twin Lakes Lake Access and Moss Creek Day Use Area come next. By now, the Kentucky Dam may be visible. Pass high bluffs then metal pillars used to hold barges just before reaching the Barkley Canal, 35 miles north of Boswell Landing. Pass through the rock-lined connector and keep along the LBL shoreline.

Land Between the Lakes
Paddle Route

Barkley Dam is visible to your left after passing through the canal. Ahead on your right is Nickell Branch Lake Access and the end of the Kentucky Lake section.

ABOUT THE SHUTTLE: To reach the take out from Exit 31 on I-24 near Lake City, head south on KY 453 for 7 miles Kentucky 453 becomes the Trace once it enters Land between the Lakes National Recreation Area. The North Welcome Station will be on your right. From the North Welcome Station at Land between the Lakes, take the Trace north 1.0 mile to Forest Road 102. Turn right on FR 102 and follow it 0.9 mile to dead-end at Nickell Branch landing. To reach the put in, backtrack to the Trace and head south on the Trace to take FR 230, Fort Henry Road. Turn right on Fort Henry Road and follow it 4.1 miles to FR 232. Turn right on FR 232 and follow it 0.1 mile to FR 233. Turn right on FR 233 and follow it 1.2 miles to dead-end at Boswell Landing.

GAUGE: This section of Kentucky Lake is floatable year-round.

LAKE BARKLEY: NICKELL BRANCH TO GATLIN POINT

class	I
gauge	Visual
level	N/A
velocity	N/A
gradient	N/A
scenery	B+

DESCRIPTION: The second portion of the LBL Paddle Route is longer—50 miles, and that is traveling in this shortest route possible with no side trips. Lake Barkley is narrower than Kentucky Lake. Long, slender islands break its lower part, potentially causing navigational problems. Getting around Kentucky Lake is simpler: head north and keep the LBL shoreline to your right. Barkley's shoreline is more continually forested with few gravel bars and fewer bluffs. The densely forested banks make finding a backcountry campsite more challenging. Look at the mouths of valleys entering the lake—they tend to offer more level ground. Be prepared to look around for a suitable campsite. However, the numerous lake accesses can always function as backup campsites. The old Cumberland River channel swings all over Lake Barkley. Barges and bigger boats often follow this channel because Barkley is riddled with shallows that normally do not affect self-propelled boats.

Begin this segment at Nickell Branch Lake Access and work east along the northern end of LBL. Large bays, like Demumbers Bay, characterize this area. Younger trees on the shoreline tell of a heavily settled area just now returning to forest. Curve north, coming to Kuttawa Lake Access at 8 miles Beyond the landing, the paddle route turns south and stays southbound for the rest of the route, shortly passing Eddyville Ferry Lake Access in a hollow. Interestingly, the big building of the Kentucky State Penitentiary lies across the lake here. Look for the water tower with "KSP" inscribed on it.

Big bays cut into LBL below Kuttawa. A portion of Cravens Bay Campground stands on the main shoreline at 17 miles. Here you can get potable water. Ahead are the first islands. The now-closed Silo Overlook on the LBL shoreline marks the Environmental Education Area. No camping is allowed in the EE Area, which is bordered on the north by Fulton Bay and on the south bay part of Taylor Bay. Be aware that camping is allowed at Taylor Bay Lake Access at mile 23.

Paddlers may want to consider entering Crooked Creek Bay, which offers good fishing and a developed campground on the far side of Energy Lake Dam. This would require a carry over the low dam. Keeping south on the now narrower main lake, reach the US 68/KY 80 bridge at 30 miles Devils Elbow Lake Access is just south of here. The shoreline remains wild for more miles below Bacon Creek Lake Access. Islands appear with regularity at this point. Smart paddlers will positively identify Neville Bay at 46 miles (you can see the grassy lake access from the main lake) and keep the LBL shoreline within view. Otherwise, you may miss the Gatlin Point Campground ramp and take-out, because several very long narrow islands block Gatlin Point from view if paddlers follow the main river channel. The Gatlin Point boat ramp, at 85 miles, marks the end of the LBL Paddle Route.

ABOUT THE SHUTTLE: To reach the put in from Exit 31 on I-24 near Lake City, head south on KY 453 for 7 miles Kentucky 453 becomes the Trace once it enters Land between the Lakes National Recreation Area. The North Welcome Station will be on your right. From the North Welcome Station at Land between the Lakes, take the Trace north 1 mile to FR 102. Turn right on FR 102 and follow it 0.9 mile to dead-end at Nickell Branch landing. To reach the Gatlin Point take out from the North Welcome Station, take the Trace south to FR 227. Turn left on FR 227 and follow it for 2 miles. Veer left on FR 229 and follow it for 1.5 miles, and the campground will be on your left. The landing is on the far side of a low dam.

GAUGE: This section of Lake Barkley is floatable year-round.

part**Ten**

STREAMS OF THE JACKSON PURCHASE

BAYOU DU CHIEN

The Bayou du Chien is a diminutive, willow- and cypress-canopied stream that flows west out of Graves County, draining southern Hickman and northern Fulton Counties before emptying into the Mississippi River. Although artificially channeled (dredged) at one time, nature has fought back over the years to reoccupy the banks with vegetation. The result is a beautiful, almost primeval little bayou that has a generally unobstructed, navigable channel.

MAPS: Water Valley, Crutchfield, Clinton, Cayce, Hickman (USGS)

KY 1283 TO KY 239

class	I
gauge	Web
level	Min. 100 Max. N/A (cfs)
velocity	0–2.5 (mph)
gradient	2.7 (fpm)
scenery	B

DESCRIPTION: Bayou du Chien runs over a mud bottom within the confines of 5-foot banks through flat farmland. At high water, the Bayou broadens from its normal 30 feet to more than a half-mile in certain places creating an immense lowland swamp and making it difficult to stay on course. At lower levels the stream can be surprisingly clear as it winds between sandbars and around logpiles. Runnable downstream of the KY 307 bridge from late fall through June, access is generally good. The level of difficulty is Class I. Dangers consist of numerous deadfalls, droves of mosquitoes, and the possibility of getting lost at higher water. The most scenic section of Bayou du Chien lies between KY 307 and KY 239. In this section particularly, wildlife abounds.

GAUGE: The USGS gauge is Bayou De Chien near Clinton. The minimum level should be 100 cfs.

Bayou du Chien

Graves Co.

Hickman Co.
Fulton Co.

Moultrie Rd.

Hodge Rd.

Clinton

Points	River Miles	Shuttle Miles
A—B	3.0	5.5
B—C	2.0	3.0
C—D	1.0	1.5
D—E	1.5	3.0
E—F	4.0	7.0

Bayou du Chien

Mud Creek

Hickman Co.
Fulton Co.

N

Obion Creek

Hickman

OBION CREEK

Obion Creek drains the south-central portion of the Jackson Purchase area in far western Kentucky. Originating at the bottom of Graves County, the creek flows over a mud bottom into Hickman and Carlisle Counties before heading southwest to empty into the Mississippi River.

MAPS: Oakton, Wolf Island, Hickman (USGS)

Points	River Miles	Shuttle Miles
A—B	3.5	5.5
B—C	6.0	8.5
C—D	2.5	3.0

US 51 TO
WHAYNES CORNER

class	I
gauge	Visual
level	Min. 3.5 ft.
	Max. N/A
velocity	0–2.5 (mph)
gradient	2.5 (fpm)
scenery	D

DESCRIPTION: Averaging 30 feet in width, Obion Creek is a dense tangle of cypress trees and deadfalls. Recommended only to those adventurous souls who don't mind paddling in a cloud of mosquitoes or portaging every 200 feet, Obion Creek offers the utmost in flatwater paddling hardship. Banks are from 5 to 8 feet high and broaden onto wide, flat floodplains forested with oak and hickory trees. The creek itself is dense with scrub vegetation and almost completely overhung with trees; primarily willows. Obion Creek is runnable (has sufficient water) from US 51 to its mouth from November to mid-June. Access is difficult at best, though the US 51 bridge isn't bad. Deadfalls and flash flooding present the greatest hazards to navigation.

GAUGE: There is a gauge on the downstream side of the US 51 bridge. Minimum reading should be 3.5 feet.

MAYFIELD CREEK

Mayfield Creek originates in Calloway County and flows northwest through Graves and McCracken Counties before becoming the Ballard–Carlisle County line and emptying into the Mississippi River south of Cairo, Illinois.

MAPS: Westplains, Hickory, Melber, Lovelaceville Blandville, Wickcliffe (USGS)

EAST OF HICKORY TO KY 121

class	I
gauge	Visual
level	Min. 160
	Max. N/A
	(cfs)
velocity	0–2.5 (mph)
gradient	3.8 (fpm)
scenery	B

DESCRIPTION: Only runnable north of the city of Mayfield, the creek is distinguished by the purity of its water and the abundance of wildlife along its banks. Flowing through flat farmland, over a sand and clay bottom beneath steep 10-foot banks, Mayfield Creek is serenely enclosed by cypress, willow, and sycamore trees and by thick scrub vegetation. The level of difficulty is Class I throughout, but sandbars and the twisting nature of the stream make paddling interesting. Averaging 35–55 feet in width, the creek can be run from just east of Hickory (north of Mayfield) downstream from late fall to early summer. Access is generally good. Dangers consist of deadfalls, beaver dams, and flash flooding that turns the floodplain into a large swamp. Paddlers who may canoe the Mayfield during hunting season are advised to wear bright clothing and attach an orange bicycle flag (on a pole) to the bow of the boat because the area is a perennial favorite of hunters. Recommended paddling sections are from east of Hickory to US 62. Numerous access points off KY 1241 make trips of varied distances easy. West of US 62, access is more difficult and the stream not nearly as pristine or beautiful.

GAUGE: Visual. Mayfield Creek is usually runnable from late fall through early summer.

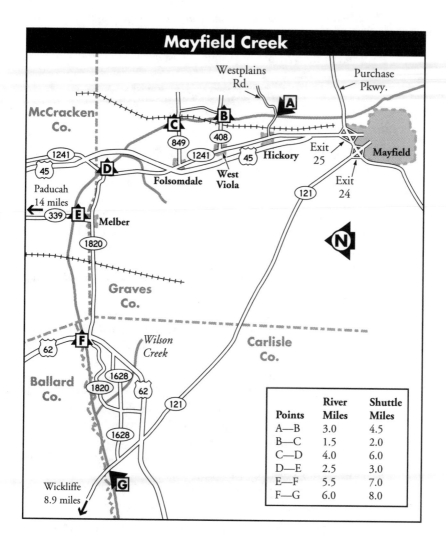

Mayfield Creek

Westplains Rd.

Purchase Pkwy.

A

McCracken Co.

C

B

849

408

1241

1241

45

Hickory

Exit 25

Mayfield

45

D

Exit 24

Paducah 14 miles

Folsomdale

West Viola

121

339 **E**

Melber

N

1820

Graves Co.

Wilson Creek

Carlisle Co.

62 **F**

1628

1820

62

Ballard Co.

121

1628

Wickliffe 8.9 miles

G

Points	River Miles	Shuttle Miles
A—B	3.0	4.5
B—C	1.5	2.0
C—D	4.0	6.0
D—E	2.5	3.0
E—F	5.5	7.0
F—G	6.0	8.0

CLARKS RIVER

The Clarks River drains Marshall, Graves, and McCracken Counties southeast of Paducah. Except for the three or four miles near Paducah, upstream of its mouth at the Tennessee River, the Clarks River is beautiful and engaging. Wildlife abounds, particularly beaver, raccoon, deer, and (during the fall) duck.

MAPS: Elva, Symsonia, Paducah East (USGS)

EAST FORK TO MOUTH OF CLARKS RIVER

class	I
gauge	Web
level	Min. 165
	Max. N/A
	(cfs)
velocity	0–2.5 (mph)
gradient	1.3 (fpm)
scenery	B

DESCRIPTION: Running through flat farm- and woodland (and through what is swamp during the rainy season), the river flows between steep mud banks crowded with cypress, sycamore, willow, maple, and scrub vegetation. The stream is exceptionally winding and continually loops back on itself. Oxbow lakes are common and are worth visiting to observe the wildlife. The Clarks River is runnable downstream of the bridge on the Sharpe-Elva Road on the East Fork, to its mouth at the Tennessee River from midfall to early summer. The West Fork of the Clarks River is not runnable. The Clarks' average width is 35–45 feet on the East Fork and 60 feet below the confluence of the forks. The level of difficulty is Class I with deadfalls and seasonal flooding posing the major dangers. On the East Fork especially, it is very easy to get lost when the river has overflowed the adjoining floodplain. Current in the upper sections is unexpectedly swift for a low-gradient stream of western Kentucky, but it halts abruptly about 6 miles upstream of the mouth where the backwater of the Tennessee River begins, around Lyndon Rd. In this same section, some powerboats are encountered, and the stream sacrifices much of its attractiveness as it approaches Paducah. Scrub vegetation, insects, and streamside private property limit canoe-camping possibilities. Access is good, but many of the access roads are dirt and gravel and are unmarked.

GAUGE: The USGS Gauge is Clarks River at Almo. The minimum reading should be 165 cfs.

Clarks River

Paducah
← 2 miles

Tennessee River

62

D

24

Lyndon
Rd.

Exit
16

62

24

131

1042

B Shady
Grove

Sharpe-
Elva Rd.

A

McCracken
Co.

450

West Fork

Graves
Co.

East Fork

N

Marshall
Co.

Points	River Miles	Shuttle Miles
A—B	5.0	6.5
B—C	6.0	4.0
C—D	5.0	4.5

part**Eleven**

WATERS OF SPECIAL MENTION

BALLARD WILDLIFE MANAGEMENT AREA

Located in Ballard County in the far northwestern corner of the state along the Ohio River, the Ballard Wildlife Management Area (BWMA) is easily one of the most unusual water resources in the state of Kentucky. Consisting of more than 15 oxbow lakes and cypress bogs, the refuge-hunting area is home to countless deer, beaver, waterfowl, songbirds, and reptiles.

MAPS: Olmstead, Barlow (USGS)

BALLARD COUNTY

class	NA
gauge	Visual
level	N/A
velocity	Lakes
gradient	N/A
scenery	A

DESCRIPTION: Captivating in its primeval beauty, sometimes ghostly and mysterious with imposing cypress standing guard over a watery carpet of lotus, the BWMA is always alive and always alluring. For the paddler, whose canoe allows exploring without restriction, the lakes of the BWMA offer unparalleled serenity and an opportunity to observe firsthand myriad forms of bird, animal, and fish life. Several well-kept, primitive camping areas designated within the BWMA serve as base camps from which the refuge can be explored. Lakes and bogs are generally separated by only a few hundred feet, so portaging from one lake to another is not difficult. All paddling is on lakes with no moving current, and motorboat traffic is light, with BWMA regulations forbidding the use of all but silent electric motors. There are no hazards to navigation. Insects and mosquitoes represent the only potential nuisance.

GAUGE: Most lakes can be paddled year-round.

Ballard Wildlife Management Area

Dam 53

Gap Cr.

Ohio River

Shelby Lake

H.Q.

473

To Monkeys Eyebrow

Little Turner Lake

Turner Lake

Turkey Lake

Goose Pond

Mitchell Lake

Gastor Lake

Butler Lake

473

Burnt Slough Lake

Bandana

Lake Slough

Mud Slough

Oak Lake

Clanton Cr.

1105

Beaver Dam Lakes

Turner Landing Rd.

Oscar

Happy Hollow Lake

Humphrey Cr.

310

To La Center

1105

To Wickliffe

To Barlow

Turner Landing

RED RIVER OF LOGAN COUNTY

Kentucky has two Red Rivers. This Red River is the north fork of the Red River of Tennessee, originating in Simpson County (KY) and Robertson County (TN). This Red River flows west along the Kentucky–Tennessee border through Logan County, ultimately returning to Tennessee, emptying into the Cumberland River near Clarksville.

MAPS: Prices Mill, Adair, Dot, Allensville (USGS)

class	I
gauge	Web
level	Min. 250 Max. flood (cfs)
velocity	2.6–5.0 (mph)
gradient	4.3 (fpm)
scenery	B

PRICES MILL TO TENNESSEE STATE LINE

DESCRIPTION: Runnable below Prices Mill from early November through mid-June, the Red River meanders through flat and rolling farm country and woodland and is not often paddled. The riverbed is of rock, sand, and clay with lushly vegetated banks of varying steepness. The stream is very tranquil, with a slow current and several varieties of trees (including sycamores) shading the water. Access is easy at the KY 591 bridge west of Adairville and also at the TN 161 bridge south of Keysburg. At the KY 591 bridge at Prices Mill, access is much improved over times past. Now a river access leads just off KY 591 on the north side of the river, down to the old mill dam just above the Prices Mill Bridge. Other access points include the KY 765 bridge and the KY 1308 bridge. The Red River averages 60–70 feet in width with occasional small islands and gravel bars dividing the river into ribbons. No obstructions other than an infrequent deadfall are in the river. It is 9 miles from Prices Mill to the KY 1308 bridge, 3 more miles to the US 431 bridge, 8 more miles to the KY 1041 bridge, and 7 more miles to the KY 102 bridge.

GAUGE: The USGS gauge is Red River at Port Royal, TN. The minimum reading should be 250 cfs for parts of the river west of Adairville and 350 cfs to run the Red east of Adairville.

Red River of Logan County

Points	River Miles	Shuttle Miles
AA—A	1.5	2.3
A—B	3.58	2.1
B—C	4.29	7.15
C—D	3.0	6.58
D—E	5.72	5.01
E—F	2.15	1.43
F—G	2.36	2.15
G—H	7.01	7.15

HARRODS CREEK OF OLDHAM
AND JEFFERSON COUNTIES

Harrods Creek originates in western Henry County and flows south-west through Oldham and Jefferson Counties before emptying into the Ohio River in northeastern Louisville.

MAPS: LaGrange, Owen, Anchorage, Jeffersonville (USGS)

KY 53 TO THE OHIO RIVER

class	I–II
gauge	Visual
level	Min. 180 Max. flood (cfs)
velocity	2.6–5.0+ (mph)
gradient	11 (fpm)
scenery	B

DESCRIPTION: Runnable from late November to early May downstream of KY 53 (and all year between the bridge at KY 329 and the Ohio River), Harrods Creek is a pleasant Class I (II) run that winds between large boulders at the bottom of an intimate, wooded gorge. In spite of ever-encroaching Louisville, the creek, averaging 25–40 feet wide, still seems secluded and almost pristine in its rugged setting. Rapids never exceed an easy Class II in difficulty (and most wash out at very high water), and dangers are limited to an occasional deadfall. Access is excellent. After heavy rains there is sometimes suffi-cient water to paddle Harrods Creek above KY 53. This is nei-ther practicable nor safe, however, due to numerous cattle gates (fences) crossing the stream. It is 5.7 miles from the KY 53 bridge to the KY 393 bridge, 7 more miles to the KY 1694 bridge, 8.5 miles farther to the KY 329 bridge, and 8.5 miles farther to the Ohio River.

GAUGE: Check Harrods Creek for runnability from November to early May and after heavy rains.

Harrods Creek

Exit 22

La Grange

53

71

Exit 18

146

393

Exit 17

22

A

42

393

B

Cedar Pt. Rd.

Exit 14

329

1817

C

71

22

1649

Ohio River

1649

329

42

D

Exit 9

841

Oldham Co.

E

Exit 37

River Rd.

Jefferson Co.

Points	River Miles	Shuttle Miles
A—B	5.72	7.29
B—C	6.86	8.72
C—D	8.51	5.72
D—E	8.44	6.44

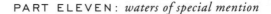

LITTLE KENTUCKY RIVER

The Little Kentucky River originates in Henry County and flows northeast, draining portions of Trimble and Carroll Counties before emptying into the Ohio River near Carrollton.

MAPS: Smithfield, Bedford, Campbellsburg (USGS)

SULPHUR TO KY 316

class	II
gauge	Visual
level	Min. 160
	Max. flood
	(cfs)
velocity	2.6–5.0
	(mph)
gradient	17 (fpm)
scenery	C

DESCRIPTION: Tree-lined with a rock and mud bottom and banks of varying steepness averaging 5 feet in height, the Little Kentucky River is runnable downstream of KY 157 from mid-November to late April or early May. The most popular section, between Sulphur and US 421, is a bouncy, Class II whitewater run when the water is up. Scenery is pleasant with rolling, grazing land flanking the stream and some occasional exposed rock cliffs. Dangers to paddlers include numerous deadfalls, a dam that must be portaged, and cattle gates. Access is good for the section recommended.

GAUGE: The river is a catch-as-catch-can proposition. Paddlers have to visually check the water before running.

OTHER PADDLING STREAMS

In addition to the streams listed here, there are several other streams that paddling enthusiasts get on when they can. However, running these streams has been problematic—they have only been run a few times and the runs are not well known, they rise and fall very rapidly after rains, or accesses have not been firmly established. That being said, adventurous "steep creekers" are discovering and making first descents of streams that may become standard paddling places in the future.

What follows are some creeks in transition. In the future they may become part of the regular circuit or the topic of tales of what could be if not for lack of water, cattle fences, unfriendly landowners, and so on. Interested paddlers can check the American Whitewater Association Web site (www.americanwhite water.org) for the latest status on these streams. Banklick Creek, a tributary of the Licking River in Kenton County, has Class II–III water, but water quality has been a problem in the past.

Little Kentucky River

Points	River Miles	Shuttle Miles
A—B	5.2	5.1
B—C	2.9	6.2

Cedar Branch, in Mercer County near the Shaker Village of Pleasant Hill, has Class III–IV water in a steep, walled gorge when it is up. It comes into the Kentucky River just upstream of old Lock 7. White Oak Creek, just off US 27 in Garrard County is reputed to be the steepest creek run in Kentucky to date. It lies within Nature Conservancy Land. The put-in is decent, but the take-out requires a 2-mile upstream paddle on the Kentucky River! White Oak Creek also holds many strainers. Glenns Creek, offering a 3-mile Class II–III run, traverses horse country near Lexington, but access is a problem. Gunpowder Creek is also a tributary of the Licking River and offers 7 miles of Class II+ water in Boone County. The beautiful creek has had water quality problems in the past. Jouett Creek, a tributary of the Kentucky River near Winchester, has an extremely small drainage —you have to practically sit in your car and watch the water to catch it at a runnable level. Rapids can be exciting and rugged because they are Class IV. Access is very limited. Roaring Paunch Creek, in the Big South Fork, has only been run a couple of times. The boulder-choked stream is very challenging, with Class IV–V+ rapids, portages, and a lot of scouting to be expected. Shawnee Run is a short creek that flows into the Kentucky River near Harrodsburg. When up, it has Class I–III (IV) rapids. It also has over ten cattle fences in 2 miles! Many smaller streams throughout the state offer Class I paddling in spring.

As the sport grows, adventurous paddlers will scout and run new streams, and other watercourses will undoubtedly be added to this list. If you are considering the just-mentioned streams or any other unknown waters, first check the AWA Web site, consult other paddlers, and assemble a team to run your creek of choice—unforeseen strainers, cattle fences, low-water bridges, and impossible rapids can turn a watery adventure into a life-or-death experience. Be a smart paddler.

Appendices

Appendix A: American Whitewater Safety Code

The American Whitewater Safety Code is perhaps the most useful overall safety guideline available. This code was most recently revised in 1998.

I. PERSONAL PREPAREDNESS AND RESPONSIBILITY

Be a competent swimmer, with the ability to handle yourself underwater.

Wear a life jacket. A snugly-fitting vest-type life preserver offers back and shoulder protection as well as the flotation needed to swim safely in whitewater.

Wear a solid, correctly fitted helmet when upsets are likely. This is essential in kayaks or covered canoes, and recommended for open canoeists using thigh straps and rafters running steep drops.

Do not boat out of control. Your skills should be sufficient to stop or reach shore before reaching danger. Do not enter a rapid unless you are reasonably sure that you can run it safely or swim it without injury.

Whitewater rivers contain many hazards which are not always easily recognized. The following are the most frequent killers.

High water. The river's speed and power increase tremendously as the flow increases, raising the difficulty of most rapids. Rescue becomes progressively harder as the water rises, adding to the danger. Floating debris and strainers make even an easy rapid quite hazardous. It is often misleading to judge the river level at the put in, since a small rise in a wide, shallow place will be multiplied many times where the river narrows. Use reliable gauge information whenever possible, and be aware that sun on snowpack, hard rain, and upstream dam releases may greatly increase the flow.

Cold. Cold drains your strength and robs you of the ability to make sound decisions on matters affecting your survival. Cold water immersion, because of the initial shock and the rapid heat loss which follows, is especially dangerous. Dress appropriately for bad weather or sudden immersion in the water. When the water temperature is less than 50 °F, a wetsuit or drysuit is essential for protection if you swim. Next best is wool or pile clothing under a waterproof shell. In this case, you should also carry waterproof matches and a change of clothing in a waterproof bag. If, after prolonged exposure, a person experiences uncontrollable shaking, loss of coordination, or difficulty speaking, he or she is hypothermic, and needs your assistance.

Strainers. Brush, fallen trees, bridge pilings, undercut rocks or anything else which allows river current to sweep through can pin boats and boaters against the obstacle. Water pressure on anything trapped this way can be overwhelming. Rescue is often extremely difficult. Pinning may occur in fast current, with little or not whitewater to warn of the danger.

Dams, weirs, ledges, reversals, holes, and hydraulics. When water drops over an obstacle, it curls back on itself, forming a strong upstream current which may be capable of holding a boat or swimmer. Some holes make for excellent sport. Others are proven killers. Paddlers who cannot recognize the difference should avoid all but the smallest holes. Hydraulics around man-made dams must be treated with utmost respect regardless of their height or the level of the river. Despite their seemingly benign appearance, they can create an almost escape-proof trap. The swimmers only exit from the "drowning machine" is to dive below the surface when the downstream current is flowing beneath the reversal.

Broaching. When a boat is pushed sideways against a rock by strong current, it may collapse and wrap. This is especially dangerous to kayak and decked canoe paddlers; these boats will collapse and the combination of indestructible hulls and tight outfitting may create a deadly trap. Even without entrapment, releasing pinned boats can be extremely time-consuming and dangerous. To avoid pinning, throw your weight downstream towards the rock. This allows the current to slide harmlessly underneath the hull.

Boating alone is discouraged. The minimum party is three people or two craft.

Have a frank knowledge of your boating ability, and don't attempt rivers or rapids which lie beyond that ability.

Develop the paddling skills and teamwork required to match the river you plan to boat. Most good paddlers develop skills gradually, and attempts to advance too quickly will compromise your safety and enjoyment.

Be in good physical and mental condition, consistent with the difficulties which may be expected. Make adjustments for loss of skills due to age, health, fitness. Any health limitations must be explained to your fellow paddlers prior to starting the trip.

Be practiced in self-rescue, including escape from an overturned craft. The Eskimo roll is strongly recommended for decked boaters who run rapids class IV or greater, or who paddle in cold environmental conditions.

Be trained in rescue skills, CPR, and first aid with special emphasis on the recognizing and treating hypothermia. It may save your friend's life.

Carry equipment needed for unexpected emergencies, including foot wear which will protect your feet when walking out, a throw rope, knife, whistle, and waterproof matches. If you wear eyeglasses, tie them on and carry a spare pair on long trips. Bring cloth repair tape on short runs, and a full repair kit on isolated rivers. Do not wear bulky jackets, ponchos, heavy boots, or anything else which could reduce your ability to survive a swim.

Despite the mutually supportive group structure described in this code, individual paddlers are ultimately responsible for their own safety, and must assume sole responsibility for the following decisions:

The decision to participate on any trip. This includes an evaluation of the expected difficulty of the rapids under the conditions existing at the time of the put-in.

The selection of appropriate equipment, including a boat design suited to their skills and the appropriate rescue and survival gear.

The decision to scout any rapid, and to run or portage according to their best judgment. Other members of the group may offer advice, but paddlers should resist pressure from anyone to paddle beyond their skills. It is also their responsibility to decide whether to pass up any walk-out or take-out opportunity.

All trip participants should consistently evaluate their own and their group's safety, voicing their concerns when appropriate and following what they believe to be the best course of action. Paddlers are encouraged to speak with anyone whose actions on the water are dangerous, whether they are a part of your group or not.

II. BOAT AND EQUIPMENT PREPAREDNESS

Test new and different equipment under familiar conditions before relying on it for difficult runs. This is especially true when adopting a new boat design or outfitting system. Low volume craft may present additional hazards to inexperienced or poorly conditioned paddlers.

Be sure your boat and gear are in good repair before starting a trip. The more isolated and difficult the run, the more rigorous this inspection should be.

Install flotation bags in noninflatable craft, securely fixed in each end, designed to displace as much water as possible. Inflatable boats should have multiple air chambers and be test inflated before launching.

Have strong, properly sized paddles or oars for controlling your craft. Carry sufficient spares for the length and difficulty of the trip.

Outfit your boat safely. The ability to exit your boat quickly is an essential component of safety in rapids. It is your responsibility to see that there is absolutely nothing to cause entrapment when coming free of an upset craft. this includes:

Spray covers which won't release reliably or which release prematurely.

Boat outfitting too tight to allow a fast exit, especially in low volume kayaks or decked canoes. This includes low hung thwarts in canoes lacking adequate clearance for your feet and kayak footbrakes which fail or allow your feet to become wedged under them.

Inadequately supported decks which collapse on a paddler's legs when a decked boat is pinned by water pressure. Inadequate clearance with the deck because of your size or build.

Loose ropes which cause entanglement. Beware of any length of loose line attached to a whitewater boat. All items must be tied tightly and excess line eliminated; painters throw lines, and safety rope systems must be completely and effectively stored. Do not knot the end of a rope, as it can get caught in cracks between rocks.

Provide ropes which permit you to hold on to your craft so that it may be rescued. the following methods are recommended:

Kayaks and covered canoes should have grab loops of 1/4" + rope or equivalent webbing sized to admit a normal sized hand. Stern painters are permissible if properly secured.

Open canoes should have securely anchored bow and stern painters consisting of 8–feet of 1/4"+ line. These must be secured in such a way that they are readily accessible, but cannot come loose accidentally. Grab loops are acceptable, but are more difficult to reach after an upset.

Rafts and dories may have taut perimeter lines threaded through the loops provided. Footholds should be designed so that a paddler's feet cannot be forced through them, causing entrapment. Flip lines should be carefully and reliably stowed.

Know your craft's carrying capacity, and how added loads affect boat handling in whitewater. Most rafts have a minimum crew size which can be added to on day trips or in easy rapids. Carrying more than two paddlers in an open canoe when running rapids is not recommended.

Car top racks must be strong and attach positively to the vehicle. Lash your boat to each crossbar, and then tie the ends of the boats directly to the bumpers for added security. This arrangement should survive all but the most violent vehicle accident.

III. GROUP PREPAREDNESS AND RESPONSIBILITY

Organization. A river trip should be regarded as a common adventure by all participants, except on instructional or commercially guided trips as defined below. Participants share the responsibility for the conduct of the trip, and each participant is individually responsible for judging his or her own capabilities and for his or her own safety as the trip progresses. Participants are encouraged (but are not obligated) to offer advice and guidance for the independent consideration and judgment of others.

River conditions. The group should have a reasonable knowledge of the difficulty of the run. Participants should evaluate this information and adjust their plans accordingly. If the run is exploratory or no one is familiar with the river, maps and guidebooks, if available, should be examined. The group should secure accurate flow information; the more difficult the run, the more important this will be. Be aware of possible changes in river level and how this will affect the difficulty of the run. If the trip involves tidal stretches, secure appropriate information on tides.

Group equipment should be suited to the difficulty of the river. The group should always have a throw line available, and one line per boat is recommended on difficult runs. The list may include: carbines, prussic loops, first-aid kit, flashlight, folding saw, fire starter, guidebooks, maps, food, extra clothing, and any other rescue or survival items suggested by conditions. Each item is not required on every run, and this list is not meant to be a substitute for good judgment.

Keep the group compact, but maintain sufficient spacing to avoid collisions. If the group is large, consider dividing into smaller groups or using the "buddy system" as an additional safeguard. Space yourselves closely enough to permit good communication, but not so close as to interfere with one another in rapids.

A point paddler sets the pace. When in front, do not get in over your head. Never run drops when you cannot see a clear route to the bottom or, for advanced paddlers, a sure route to the next eddy. When in doubt, stop and scout.

Keep track of all group members. Each boat keeps the one behind it in sight, stopping if necessary. Know how many people are in your group and take head counts regularly. No one should paddle ahead or walk out without first informing the group. Paddlers requiring additional support should stay at the center of a group, and not allow themselves to lag behind in the more difficult rapids. If the group is large and contains a wide range of abilities, a sweep boat may be designated to bring up the rear.

Courtesy. On heavily used rivers, do not cut in front of a boater running a drop. Always look upstream before leaving eddies to run or play. Never enter a crowded drop or eddy when no room for you exists. Passing other groups in a rapid may be hazardous: it's often safer to wait upstream until the group ahead has passed.

Float plan. If the trip is into a wilderness area or for an extended period, plans should be filed with a responsible person who will contact the authorities if you are overdue. It may be wise to establish checkpoints along the way where civilization could be contacted if necessary. Knowing the location of possible help and preplanning escape routes can speed rescue.

Drugs. The use of alcohol or mind altering drugs before or during river trips is not recommended. It dulls reflexes, reduces decision making ability, and may interfere with important survival reflexes.

Instructional or commercially guided trips. in contrast to the common adventure trip format, in these trip formats, a boating instructor or commercial guide assumes some of the responsibilities normally exercised by the group as a whole, as appropriate under the circumstances. These formats recognize that instructional or commercially guided trips may involve participants who lack significant experience in whitewater. However, as a participant acquires experience in whitewater, he or she takes on increasing responsibility for his or her own safety, in accordance with what he or she knows or should know as a result of that increased experience. Also, as in all trip formats, every participant must realize and assume the risks associated with the serious hazards of whitewater rivers. it is advisable for instructors and commercial guides or their employers to acquire trip or personal liability insurance:

An "instructional trip" is characterized by a clear teacher/pupil relationship, where the primary purpose of the trip is to teach boating skills, and which is conducted for a fee.

A "commercially guided trip" is characterized by a licensed, professional guide conducting trips for a fee.

IV. GUIDELINES FOR RIVER RESCUE

Recover from an upset with an Eskimo roll whenever possible. Evacuate your boat immediately if there is imminent danger of being trapped against rocks, brush, or any other kind of strainer.

If you swim, hold on to your boat. It has much flotation and is easy for rescuers to spot. Get to the upstream end so that you cannot be crushed between a rock and your boat by the force of the current. Persons with good balance may be able to climb on top of a swamped kayak or flipped raft and paddle to shore.

Release your craft if this will improve your chances, especially if the water is cold or dangerous rapids lie ahead. Actively attempt self-rescue whenever possible by swimming for safety. Be prepared to assist others who may come to your aid.

When swimming in shallow or obstructed rapids, lie on your back with feet held high and pointed downstream. Do not attempt to stand in fast moving water; if your foot wedges on the bottom, fast water will push you under and keep you there. Get to slow or very shallow water before attempting to stand or walk. Look ahead! Avoid possible pinning situations including under-cut rocks, strainers, downed trees, holes, and other dangers by swimming away from them.

If the rapids are deep and powerful, roll over onto your stomach and swim aggressively for shore. Watch for eddies and slack-water and use them to get out of the current. Strong swimmers can affect a powerful upstream ferry and get to shore fast. If the shores are obstructed with strainers or under cut rocks, however, it is safer to ride the rapid out" until a safer escape can be found.

If others spill and swim, go after the boaters first. Rescue boats and equipment only if this can be done safely. While participants are encouraged (but not obligated) to assist one another to the best of their ability, they should do so only if they can, in their judgment, do so safely. The first duty of a rescuer is not to compound the problem by becoming another victim.

The use of rescue lines requires training; uninformed use may cause injury. Never tie yourself into either end of a line without a reliable quick-release system. Have a knife handy to deal with unexpected entanglement. Learn to place set lines effectively, to throw accurately, to belay, and to properly handle a rope thrown to you.

When reviving a drowning victim, be aware that cold water may greatly extend survival time underwater. Victims of hypothermia may have depressed vital signs so they look and feel dead. Don't give up; continue CPR for as long as possible without compromising safety.

Appendix B: Outfitters

Canoe Kentucky
7323 Peaks Mill Road
Frankfort, KY 40601
(800) K-CANOE-1
www.canoeky.com

Operates primarily on the Elkhorn River system but also has trips on the Green and will do special trips all over the state.

Green River Canoes
209 Southside Drive
Campbellsville, KY
(270) 789-2956

Mike Dougherty serves the Green River from below Green Lake to Munfordville. His featured trip is the Roachville Run. Call ahead for service. He also handles custom group trips.

Green River Canoeing
1145 Main Street
Brownsville, KY 42210
(270) 597-2031

They operate on the Green River between Munfordville and Houchins Ferry, including the Green through Mammoth Cave National Park. They also run trips on the Nolin from below Nolin River Lake to the Green. Their trips last from two hours to two days.

Kentucky Kayak Kountry
2040 J. H. O'Bryan Drive
Grand Rivers, KY 42045
(270) 362-0087

This outfit, open April through October, offers guided and unguided kayak trips along the Little River, the Muddy Fork Little River, and the bays of Land Between the Lakes.

Mammoth Cave Canoe & Kayak
1240 Old Mammoth Cave Road
Cave City, KY 42127
(877) 592-2663
www.mammothcavecanoe-k.com

Licensed to operate in Mammoth Cave National Park, they offer canoe trips on the Green River lasting from three hours to three days.

Red River Outdoors
415 Natural Bridge Road
Slade, KY 40376
(606) 663-9701
www.redriveroutdoors.com

Centered on the Red River Gorge, they offer canoe trips on various parts of the Red, rock climbing, and shuttle services for paddlers and backpackers.

Rockcastle Adventures Canoe Livery
Box 662
London, KY 40441
(606) 864-9407

Rents canoes and offers shuttle service on Rockcastle and other local lakes and rivers.

Sheltowee Trace Outfitters
P.O. Box 1060
Whitley City, KY 42653
(800) 541-RAFT
www.ky-rafting.com

Located near Cumberland Falls State Park, this group offers canoes, kayaks, and rafts along with guided and unguided trips on the Big South Fork, Cumberland River, and Russell Fork.

Still Waters Canoe Trail
249 Strohmeier Road
Frankfort, KY 40601
(502) 223-8896

Located near the confluence of Elkhorn Creek and the Kentucky River near Frankfort, they offer trips on both the Elkhorn and the Kentucky River.

Thaxton's Licking River Canoe Rental
33 Hornbeek Road Suite 3
Butler, KY 412006
(859) 472-2000
www.gopaddling.com

Jim Thaxton and company offer day and overnight trips on the Licking River, as well as overnight trips on the South Fork Licking River.

Appendix C: Clubs

KENTUCKY CLUBS

Bluegrass Whitewater Association
P.O. Box 4231
Lexington, KY 4231
www.surfbwa.org

Viking Canoe Club
P.O. Box 32263
Louisville, KY
www.vikingcanoeclub.org

NATIONAL CLUBS

American Canoe Association
7432 Alban Station Boulevard, Suite B 232
Springfield, VA 22150
(703) 451-0141
www.acnet.org

American Whitewater Association
1424 Fenwick Lane
Silver Spring, MD 20910
(866) BOAT4AW
www.americanwhitewater.org

Appendix D: Glossary

Back band (back rest): Provides support for the lower back while kayaking and helps with erect posture in the boat. Located behind the seat and usually made of padded fabric, plastic, or foam.

Blade: The broad part at the ends of the paddle.

Bow: The forward end of the boat.

Bulkhead: A cross-sectional wall inside a kayak, made of composite, plastic, or foam. Bulkheads provide structural support and, if sealed around the inside of the hull, can create watertight compartments for buoyancy and storage. They are sometimes also used as foot braces.

Cockpit: The enclosed central compartment on a kayak, in which the paddler sits.

Deck: The top part of a kayak that keeps the hull from filling with water.

Flotation: Waterproof compartments, foam blocks, or inflatable airbags. Flotation will help a swamped boat stay on the surface, making rescue and reentry easier.

Foot pegs (foot braces): Usually adjustable structures inside the cockpit on which a kayaker places the balls of his feet. See Bulkhead.

Hull: The structural body of the boat, the shape of which determines how the boat will perform in various conditions.

PFD: Personal flotation device. Cushions, floats, and, most importantly for kayakers, lifejackets. PFDs used in the United States must be approved by the U.S. Coast Guard and must be worn to be effective. The Coast Guard recognizes five classes of PFDs. The ACA recommends kayakers use Class III PFDs in most situations.

Rocker: The amount of curvature of a line down the middle of a kayaks hull, from bow to stern. More rocker (more curvature) usually makes a kayak more maneuverable. Less rocker tends to help the kayak track in a straight line.

Roll: The technique of righting a capsized kayak with the paddler remaining in the paddling position.

Shaft: The long, skinny part of a kayak paddle.

Sit-on-top: Kayaks without a cockpit, sit-on-tops are usually self-bailing with various seat and foot-brace configurations. Many are for recreational use, but some are designed for touring and racing.

Spray skirt (spray deck): A neoprene or nylon skirt worn by a kayaker that attaches to the rim of the cockpit. It keeps water out of the kayak.

Stern: The rear end of the kayak.

Swamp: To fill (a kayak) with water.

Thigh braces (knee braces): Usually found in whitewater and touring kayaks, these structures inside the cockpit give the paddler points of contact important for boat control.

Trim: The bow-to-stern leveling of a kayak that affects boat control. In most cases it should be nearly level, or with the stern slightly lower in the water.

Wet exit: Coming out of a capsized kayak.

Index

About the Authors

Johnny Molloy is an outdoor writer based in Tennessee. A native Tennessean, he was born in Memphis and moved to Knoxville in 1980 to attend the University of Tennessee. In Knoxville he developed his love of the natural world that has since become the primary focus his life.

It all started on a backpacking foray into the Great Smoky Mountains National Park. That first trip, though a disaster, unleashed an innate love of the outdoors that has led to his spending over 100 nights in the wild per year over the past 20 years, backpacking and canoe camping throughout our country and abroad. In 1987, after graduating from the University of Tennessee with a degree in economics, he continued to spend ever-increasing amounts of time in the natural places, becoming more skilled in a variety of environments. Friends enjoyed his adventure stories, and one even suggested he write a book. Soon he parlayed his love of the outdoors into an occupation.

The results of his efforts are over 20 books, ranging from hiking guides to paddling guides to camping guides to true outdoor adventure stories. His books primarily cover the Southeast but range to Colorado and Wisconsin. He has written several Kentucky guidebooks, including *Best in Tent Camping: Kentucky & Tennessee, Land Between the Lakes Outdoor Recreation Handbook,* and *Hiking Guide to the Sheltowee Trace National Recreation Trail* in addition to this guidebook.

Molloy has also written numerous magazine articles for magazines such as *Backpacker* and *Sea Kayaker*. He also has written for Web sites such as gorp.com.

He continues to write to this day and travels extensively to all four corners of the United States endeavoring in a variety of outdoor pursuits.

Bob Sehlinger, author of seven paddling guides and dozens of travel books, is the former president of the Eastern Professional River Outfitters Association. He also served as program director for the SAGE, Inc. school of the outdoors. A native of the southeastern states, Bob has led canoeing trips throughout eastern North America from the rivers of northern Ontario, Canada, to the bayous of Louisiana. He is the publisher of Menasha Ridge Press and resides with his family in Birmingham, Alabama.